GLOB

GW00326604

The best of

KUALA
LUMPUR

SEAN SHEEHAN

NEW
HOLLAND

GLOBETROTTER™

Second edition published in 2008
by New Holland Publishers (UK) Ltd
London • Cape Town • Sydney • Auckland
10 9 8 7 6 5 4 3 2 1

website: www.newhollandpublishers.com

Garfield House, 86 Edgware Road
London W2 2EA
United Kingdom

80 McKenzie Street
Cape Town 8001
South Africa

Unit 1, 66 Gibbes Street,
Chatswood, NSW 2067
Australia

218 Lake Road
Northcote, Auckland
New Zealand

Distributed in the USA by
The Globe Pequot Press, Connecticut

Copyright © 2008 in text: Sean Sheehan
Copyright © 2008 in maps: Globetrotter
Travel Maps
Copyright © 2008 in photographs:
Individual photographers as credited (right)
Copyright © 2008 New Holland Publishers
(UK) Ltd

All rights reserved. No part of this publication
may be reproduced, stored in a retrieval system
or transmitted, in any form or by any means,
electronic, mechanical, photocopying, recording
or otherwise, without the prior written permis-
sion of the publishers and copyright holders.

ISBN 978 1 84537 993 3

Publishing Manager: Thea Grobbelaar
DTP Cartographic Manager: Genené Hart
Editors: Carla Zietsman, Thea Grobbelaar
Designer: Nicole Bannister
Cartographers: Carryck Wise, Elmari Kuyler
Picture Researcher: Shavonne Govender

Reproduction by Resolution (Cape Town)
Printed and bound by Times Offset (M) Sdn. Bhd.,
Malaysia.

Although every effort has been made to ensure
that this guide is up to date and current at time
of going to print, the Publisher accepts no
responsibility or liability for any loss, injury or
inconvenience incurred by readers or travellers
using this guide.

Photographic Credits:
Alamy/Royal Geographical Society: page 8;
Gerald Cubitt: pages 11, 16, 27, 32, 44, 47,
71, 79, 80, 81, 82, 83;
NHIL/Ryno Reyneke: title page, pages 6, 7,
10, 12, 13, 14, 15, 17, 18, 19, 20, 21, 22, 23,
24, 25, 26, 28, 29, 30, 31, 33, 34, 36, 37, 39,
40, 41, 42, 45, 46, 48, 49, 50, 53, 54, 60 (top
and bottom), 62, 65, 66, 69, 70, 74, 76, 84;
Pictures Colour Library: cover;
Sean Sheehan: pages 38, 43;
Travel Ink/Abbie Enock: page 75;
Travel Ink/Allan Hartley: pages 73, 78;
Travel Ink/Walter Wolfe: page 9.
[NHIL=New Holland Image Library]

Front Cover: *Petronas Towers, with the city in
the foreground.*
Title Page: *Craft shops in Kuala Lumpur display
artefacts from around the country, from hand-
blocked kites to batik clothing.*

CONTENTS

MAKE THE MOST OF YOUR GUIDE

Reading these two pages will help you to get the most out of your guide and save you time when using it. Sites discussed in the text are cross-referenced with the cover maps – for example, the reference 'Map B–C3' refers to the Kuala Lumpur Map (Map B), column C, row 3. Use the Map Plan below to quickly locate the map you need.

MAP PLAN

Outside Back Cover   Outside Front Cover

Inside Front Cover   Inside Back Cover

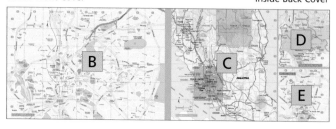

THE BIGGER PICTURE

Key to Map Plan

A – Kuala Lumpur and
    Surrounds
B – Kuala Lumpur
C – Excursions
D – Taman Negara
E – Melaka
F – Cameron Highlands
G – Kuala Lumpur Transit
    Map

USING THIS BOOK

Key to Symbols

⊠ — address

☎ — telephone

℘ — fax

🖳 — website

🖰 — e-mail address

⊕ — opening times

🚌 — transport

💰 — entry fee

🍽 — restaurants nearby

Map Legend

motorway		main road	Kuching
national road		other road	C. de Sant Pau
main road		golf course	⌐
minor road		built-up area	
river	Pahang	post office	⊠
route number	N340	building of interest	Petronas Twin Towers
city	KUALA LUMPUR	museum	Youth Museum
major town	⊙ Seremban	parking area	P
town	O Kajang	hospital	⊕
village	◎ Kuala Rompin	shopping centre	Kuala Lumpur Plaza ⑤
peaks in metres	Gn. Nuang ▲ 1493 m	metro station	● Kampung Bahru
railway		place of worship	△ Church △ Mosque 🛕 Temple
place of interest	★ National Art Gallery	police station	●
airport	✈	tourist information	ℹ
camp	⌂ Nusa Camp	park & garden	Parc del Migdia
		hotel	Ⓗ MANDARIN

Keep us Current

Travel information is apt to change, which is why we regularly update our guides. We'd be most grateful to receive feedback from you if you've noted something we should include in our updates. If you have any new information, please share it with us by writing to the Publishing Manager, Globetrotter, at the office nearest to you (addresses on the imprint page of this guide). The most significant contribution to each new edition will be rewarded with a free copy of the updated guide.

Above: *Surrounded by low-lying hills, KL is dominated by the Petronas Towers.*

KUALA LUMPUR

Kuala Lumpur is a new city, founded in the middle of the 19th century as a mining town. It lay relatively dormant for a hundred years or so, slowly accreting bits and pieces – a row of shophouses here, a mosque or tall building there – then suddenly it burst into Pacific Tiger development, sprouting hotels and shopping centres and record-breaking towers. The modern city is a confusing place – no city centre, a hotchpotch of architectural styles, traffic problems that would try the patience of a Buddha, all set in a debilitating heat and humidity – but well worth the experience for the fascinating combinations of old and new, laid back and buzzing, concrete and liana, superstition and science, the tacky and the elegant that lie side by side on every *jalan*, *pasar* and *lebuh*. Most impressive and intriguing of all, Kuala Lumpur is a strongly multicultural and tolerant city, with sizeable Chinese and Indian minorities and distinct ethnic areas.

Kuala Lumpur – everyone calls it KL – is a city to shop in. It draws in sophisticated Singaporeans for its bargains and western tourists for its crafts and specialist shops. Night markets selling strange ingredients and stranger snacks do as much business as the big glamorous shopping centres.

Above all, people come to KL to enjoy the food. From street hawkers to five-star cuisine, local *murtabaks* to flown-in steaks and rhubarb, there is so much to refresh the palate that it would take a long stay to do justice to the variety of cuisines.

Earning its Name

Kuala Lumpur translates into English as 'muddy confluence' and sort of fell into its name by default rather than a conscious effort. It was what the Chinese tin prospectors sent by Rajah Abdullah of Selangor must have grumbled to each other in 1857 as they fought their way through the malaria-infested jungle to the place where the Klang and Gombak rivers meet. The muddy confluence proved profitable since a little inland, at the place they named Ampang, great tin deposits were found, establishing the river confluence as a major staging post in the extraction of the metal. This didn't do the original prospectors much good since two thirds of them caught malaria and died.

The Land

Kuala Lumpur lies at the southwestern end of a series of north-south mountain ranges, about halfway down Malaysia's west coast and 35km (21.7 miles) inland. The city sits in a slightly murky plain surrounded by forest-covered mountains, which form the playground for city folk in their leisure time. The city itself has a few green spaces – the Lake Gardens to the west and Lake Titiwangsa to the north – but bougainvilleas and palm trees sprout from every pavement to add colour to the urban sprawl. In the very heart of the city the 20.2ha (50-acre) KLCC Park has been constructed from the old Selangor Turf Club, and KLers enjoy this green spot.

Climate

A stone's throw from the equator, Kuala Lumpur has no seasons as such. Every day in KL offers the same profusion of flowers, deep shade and sweltering heat. Even the streetside coffee shops in Bukit Bintang have free-standing air conditioners blasting out icy air to cool their customers. Daytime temperatures are 27–32°C (80–90°F) with constant high humidity, and it's no use waiting for the evening for things to cool down – they don't.

History in Brief

Kuala Lumpur's history began in 1857 when the search for tin – its value rocketing with the invention of canning – sent some immigrant Chinese tin miners into the swampy jungle seeking their fortunes. Most just found an early death but

Rainy City

The rainy season, which can shut down areas of the east coast for days between December and February, barely registers in the city but as heat and humidity build up each day there is more often than not a vast and welcome thundery downpour in the early afternoon. This can be brief but cathartic, clearing the air, washing all manner of things away into the big storm drains and bringing a brief sweaty coolness to the city. Moped riders lurk under flyovers and the coffee shops suddenly burst with customers. Rainmacs just make you hot while umbrellas are of little use – get inside somewhere, enjoy the local chatter and wait out the storm.

Below: *Peaceful Lake Titiwangsa offers a calm outlook on the city.*

Yap Ah Loy
A penniless migrant, he arrived in the peninsula at the age of 17 and went to Kuala Lumpur to earn money from mining. He became Kapitan China at the age of 30 in 1868, a post he held for the following 17 years, growing rich and powerful. At first he governed the Chinese mineworkers with a contingent of six irregulars. His methods were reputedly harsh – he executed repeat offenders – but the stability he brought to the town increased tin production and drew ever more people.

Below: *British administrators pose for a family photograph in Malaya.*

those who survived set up a staging post at the confluence of the Klang and Gombak rivers. What was to become the capital of Malaysia was then an anonymous spot in the sultanate of Selangor, ruled by Rajah Abdullah and watched over from a distance by the British in the Straits Settlements of Singapore, Melaka and Penang.

Chinese miners flooded into the area and within 10 years the confluence of the two rivers was a thriving if lawless place. Chinese clans and secret societies began to fight for control of the tin deposits. The rajah and the British tolerated the mayhem as long as profits rolled out and no other colonial powers interfered. The Chinese were governed by a headman known as the Kapitan China and it was one of these, Yap Ah Loy (*see* panel, this page), who brought a form of government to the town.

In 1867, civil war had broken out between Selangor's Malay chieftains for control of the river ports where the tin was brought from the interior. The merchants of Kuala

Lumpur got their tin out in the safest way they could, often avoiding the river ports. This dried up the profits which the chieftains were fighting over and focussed the attention of the warring parties on the town itself. In 1872 Kuala Lumpur was seized by an alliance of Malay chiefs and burned to the ground.

The following year the city was reclaimed by forces friendly to Yap Ah Loy and Yap began rebuilding the town – taking out a personal loan to do so – and encouraging miners to stay until mining could begin again. With a new hike in tin prices the town boomed once again and in 1879 the British considered it important enough to establish their presence there.

Kuala Lumpur began to blossom. Mud streets of wooden houses lined the river banks. Chinese miners were joined by Malay farmers (who provided food for the town) and eventually by British venture capitalists who were never far away from a money-making enterprise.

Above: *The National Monument in the Lake Gardens.*

Yap Ah Loy was by now a powerful man. In 1880 Kuala Lumpur became the state capital of Selangor and in 1882 the British resident arrived in the person of Frank Swettenham. A fire in 1881 had destroyed many of the town's wooden buildings and Swettenham decided to rebuild in brick. Brickworks were set up and within a decade there were hundreds of brick buildings and the population of the city increased tenfold. By the turn of the century rubber plantations were established, swelling the city's population even further and bringing the first Indian immigrants from Tamil Nadu. Roads and eventually railroads were begun. The city had changed from a small wild west town of Chinese tin miners to a multicultural capital city in the space of 50 years.

In 1896 the Federation of Malay States was created, consisting of Selangor, Perak, Negeri Sembilan and Pahang and ruled by the British with the aid of regional rulers. In 1909

British Residents
As demand for tin was booming worldwide the various states of the Malay Peninsula were fighting to control its sources. Until this time the British had been content to sit back and rake in their share of the profits from their strongholds of the Straits Settlements, but they deemed it necessary to intervene when hostilities escalated. A system of British residents was set up, the resident of each state acting in an 'advisory' capacity to the local sultan. When the sultans realized they had relinquished more power than they wanted, they rebelled. In Selangor the rebellion was ended by British troops who brought an end to civil war between the local chieftains and established some order in the state.

Kelantan, Terrenganu, Kedah and Perlis came under British authority and in 1914 Johor accepted British rule, bringing the entire peninsula under British authority. KL boomed, with a major reconstruction in 1926 of the banks of the river Klang preventing flooding and making it more navigable.

World War I left the city untouched but the next outbreak of war had drastic effects. In 1942 the Japanese, invading from the northeast, raced through the Malay Peninsula, driving disorganized Allied troops before them. As the Allies retreated out of KL, Japanese bombs rained down and stores were looted. The Chinese tin millionaires feared the arrival of the Japanese. The end of the war in 1945 saw the British back in the city but now confronted by an emerging Malay nationalism and Chinese communism. The years 1948 to 1956 were known as the Emergency and, while KL remained relatively safe from the guerrilla attacks of the insurgent Chinese, there was little development.

Malayan independence came in 1957 but antagonism between Chinese and Malays, the violence of the Emergency and Malay reluctance to accept the Chinese as equals led to riots in the city in 1969. Steps were taken to reduce Malay resentment at their economic dependence on the Chinese and the city became peaceful once again.

The 1990s saw the start of KL's awesome growth spurt and the creation of many of its modern attractions.

The New Economic Policy

The Malays resented the fact that the economy was largely dominated by the Chinese. Riots broke out in 1969 when hundreds of people – mostly Chinese – were killed. To end the violence and encourage Malay participation in the economy, the new government introduced the New Economic Policy. Malays and Orang Asli, the indigenous people of the peninsula, were designated *bumiputra* which translates as 'sons of the soil'. *Bumiputra* meant subsidized housing, grants for study abroad, and a legal requirement for every business over a certain size to have a *bumiputra* on its board.

Government and Economy

The turnaround in Malaysia's economic position began as far back as 1981 when **Mahathir Mohammed** was elected prime minister. He took a stagnating economy and enlivened it with huge engineering projects, major privatization of industries such as water, power, telecommunications, the post, railways, the national airline and road building. **Foreign investment** flooded in and the stock market soared. Malaysia changed from being a producer of primary products to an important manufacturer of goods for export; by the early 1990s Malaysia was one of the fastest growing economies in the world. The sudden economic downturn of that decade, however, became visible everywhere in KL with abandoned building projects littering the city. Now, though, in the 21st century, the economy is strong once again, projects are nearing completion and the huge developments in **Cyberjaya** and **Putrajaya**, the high-tech and administrative centres, are designed to be mini-cities in themselves.

> **Protons**
> In 1985 Malaysia became the first country in Southeast Asia to develop and manufacture its own car. The venture, in conjunction with Mitsubishi of Japan, has proved phenomenally successful. The Proton now dominates the domestic market and is also exported to more than a dozen countries around the world.

Opposite: *In the centre of the oldest part of the city, Merdeka Square proudly displays the country's flag.*
Below: *A shy Orang Asli girl poses for the camera.*

The People

Kuala Lumpur is a city of around 4.1 million people, most of them living in the satellite towns that have sprung up in the suburban areas of Selangor. Its racial mix is slightly different to the national average, with few representatives of the **Orang Asli** (the indigenous people of Malaysia) in the city. The **Chinese** form a higher proportion of KL's population than the national average, as do the **Indians**.

OVERVIEW

Peranakan
An interesting racially mixed group are the Peranakan, the descendants of mixed marriages between Chinese settlers and local women. In the city there are very few people who identify themselves as Peranakan, but the wonderful food which the mixture of cultures produced has become increasingly fashionable in the city and is well worth seeking out.

Malays form about 44% of the population of greater KL. They are thought to have originated from Sumatran tribes called the **Orang Laut** (sea people) and have been **Muslim** since the 15th century. Traditionally farmers and fishermen, their culture still is based around the courtly society with the state sultans at the head of a social hierarchy. Outside of the city many Malay people still live the traditional *kampung* (village) life with wooden houses built up on platforms and a small patch of land with coconut palms and bananas. In the *kampung* men wear a sarong while in the city they dress in suits. The women choose to wear the long smock over a full-length sarong skirt, and many wear the headdress.

KL's **Chinese** population are descendants of people who came here in the 9th century in search of a better life. They are a vital part of the city's economic health. The traditions of a much older civilization are evident among Malaysian Chinese – architects and shopkeepers alike pay attention to feng shui and Chinese festivals are keenly observed both in the back streets of Chinatown and in the most sophisticated high-rise blocks.

Below: *All dressed up for a religious festival, these Hindu people form a colourful part of the national identity.*

Indians came to Malaysia in the 19th century, mainly from southern India, to work in construction and on plantations. In the KL area they make up 18% of the population, a higher proportion than the national average. Nationally, 80% of all Tamil or south Indian Malaysians are manual workers. In the city many Indians work in cafés and restaurants serving Indian food. Many have also entered the medical and legal profession. The Hindu festival of *Thaipusam* is celebrated in the city and *Deepavali* is a national holiday.

12

KL is also home to smaller numbers of other ethnic groups. There is a sizeable **European** community of ex-patriates. Less visible, in KL at least, are the ethnically mixed groups known as **Eurasian** and **Peranakan** (*see* panel, page 12). Eurasians are descended from Portuguese, Dutch and English colonists whose family names such as De Souza or Sequeria have survived. In the city they are indistinguishable from their neigh-bours. In one area of the country, Melaka, an ancient Portuguese lan-guage called Cristão is still spoken.

Above: *Some of the beautifully hand-crafted designs in pewter available in Kuala Lumpur.*

Arts and Crafts

In the city there are many opportunities to browse through some of Malaysia's tradi-tional arts and crafts. Native to the area is **pewter** making and the Royal Selangor Factory has both a museum and a shop sell-ing handcrafted pewter items. Crafts from other regions of the country which can be seen in the city include **metalwork**, **fabrics** and **pottery**. From Kota Bahru in the north-east comes finely crafted silver filigree **jewellery** and from Terrenganu, also in the northeast, **silk brocade**, woven with silver and gold thread. From Borneo comes woven and tie-dyed cloth; the ubiquitous hand-blocked Malay **batik** (*see* panel, this page) comes chiefly from the east coast. Less com-mon in KL but well worth looking out for is the black and white **pottery**, intricate **bas-ketwork** and beautifully carved **wooden figures** from Sabah and Sarawak. **Kites** and **drums** from the northeast of the peninsula are also available in the city.

Batik

Batik originated in the islands of Indonesia but has become part of the national fabric of Malaysia. It is often seen in the formal wear of government ministers, on the uniforms of the national airline, and is ubiquitous in the hotels and restaurants of the city. Batik is made into cushions, tablecloths, clothes, even shoes and handbags. It is made by hand drawing or block-ing complex patterns onto cotton cloth with wax and then dyeing it. The wax is boiled away afterwards.

HIGHLIGHTS

The Central Market
✉ Jln. Hang Kasturi
☎ 2031 9399
💻 www.
centralmarket.com.my
🕐 11:00–22:00 (for
performances check at
the Tourist Centre)
💰 Admission is free.
🚍 Putra Line Pasar
Seni LRT

Masjid Jamek
✉ Jalan Tun Perak
☎ 2691 2829
🕐 Daily between
prayers
💰 Admission is free.
🚍 Putra/Star Line
Masjid Jamek LRT

Opposite: *The minarets and onion domes of Masjid Jamek, set among the busy roads and gleaming sky-scrapers of the city.*
Below: *The geometric shapes and clean lines of the old Central Market which offers all the arts and crafts of Malaysia under one roof.*

See Map B–D4 ★★★

THE CENTRAL MARKET

This is the heart of tourist KL. Built in 1936, this Art Deco building was the city's central wetmarket, selling all manner of live and wriggling things. In the late 1980s it was closed down, the traders moved off and the building was condemned. After a long campaign, a new plan was made to create the equivalent of England's Covent Garden here with artists, cafés and a cultural centre. The old building became the heart of the new, culturally sophisticated Kuala Lumpur.

Now pedestrianized, the area around the old market is still home to some unreconstructed coffee shops and spice grinders. Inside, the layout was designed to be as much like the old wetmarket as possible, with 120 tiny shops let to various businesses. The market has craft shops, fortune tellers, portrait painters and antiques. Upstairs are some useful places to eat and drink. There are no easy bargains to be had here but it's a good place to look for what takes your fancy. In the surrounding rows of shops are more curio stalls and artists' workshops. There is often a free cultural show of some kind going on here, especially in the evenings, and it is a grand place for people-watching. Come here to buy funny T-shirts, designer trainers or even hand-carved ornaments and blowpipes of the Orang Asli, but be prepared to bargain hard for what you want.

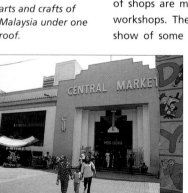

See Map B–D4	★★★

MASJID JAMEK

Heading north along the river brings you to the historically significant confluence of the rivers Klang and Gombak and here, at one of the noisiest road and rail junctions in the city, is KL's prettiest and most homely **mosque**, Masjid Jamek. It is the city's oldest surviving mosque. Built on a site that was once a Malay cemetery, it was financed by public subscription and by government funding. It was completed in

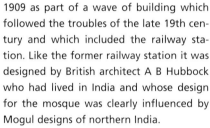

1909 as part of a wave of building which followed the troubles of the late 19th century and which included the railway station. Like the former railway station it was designed by British architect A B Hubbock who had lived in India and whose design for the mosque was clearly influenced by Mogul designs of northern India.

The colourful walls of the mosque – red brick and white marble stripes – surround a peaceful central courtyard with marble floors shaded by coconut palms. Curved steps lead right down to the water's edge. The prayer hall itself is topped by three domes, the central one 21.3m (69.8ft) high. An Arabian Nights fantasy of minarets marks the corners. You can look down into the mosque from the walkway above, or you can visit it between prayer times. Until the construction of the National Mosque in 1965 this was the centre of Muslim worship in the city.

> **Malay Religion**
> Islam came to Malaysia with south Indian traders after the 15th century and was gradually absorbed into the culture of the small kingdoms that ruled the peninsula, gradually replacing Hinduism as the dominant religion. Virtually all ethnic Malays are Muslim. Wives or husbands who are not Muslim must convert, and abandoning the religion is considered a crime. Malaysian Islam is not fundamentalist although Malays take their religion very seriously. Except during prayer times you will be welcomed at the mosque.

Below: *Looking like a fairy-tale castle, the Sultan Abdul Samad building dominates Merdeka Square.*

◎ *See* Map B–C4   ★★★

MERDEKA SQUARE

Around the confluence of the two rivers that flow through the city grew up the early municipal buildings of colonial Malaya. West of the Jamek Mosque on the west bank of the River Klang is Merdeka Square, the heart of colonial life and the symbol of independent Malaysia.

Standing on the **Padang**, the large green open space where colonials once met in the cool of the evening, you can see on the western side of the square the **Royal Selangor Club**, founded in 1884. Originally a simple timber building built in the northeast corner of the Padang, it was a social and cricket club, strictly for white men only. Rebuilt around 1890 to a design by A C Norman, the British government engineer who also built many other colonial buildings, it became a more substantial, though still a wooden, two-storey building. The mock Tudor look arrived in its third incarnation in 1910. Its nickname in those days was the 'Spotted Dog' after a pet that spent a lot of time tied up on its steps while its owner was inside sipping stengahs.

Opposite the Royal Selangor Club (still almost as exclusive now as it was in 1910, though now in terms of the city's multiracial elite) are some more of Norman's designs. Across Jalan Rajah stands the **Sultan Abdul Samad building**, erected in the 1890s as the State Secretariat, now the Supreme and High Courts. This and the other buildings

---

A Focal Point
To the south of the Padang is the paved Merdeka Square itself, its 95m (310ft) flagpole the highest in the world. Huge screens are erected here for football matches and concerts, and on Hari Merdeka the great parade is held here.

Royal Selangor Club
✉ Merdeka Square
☎ 60 3 292 7166
🚍 Putra/Star line Masjid Jamek LRT
♿ The club is not open to the public.

MERDEKA SQUARE

See Map B–C4   ★★★

which make up Merdeka Square – the **National Museum of History** (*see* page 37), formerly the government offices, and the **Infokraf building**, formerly the Department of Public Works – are all in the same strange eclectic style based on north Indian, Spanish, Venetian and Moorish styles to create a Disneyland of onion domes, pink-and-white striped walls, minarets and colonnades. Come at night when the road is closed to traffic and city dwellers come to enjoy the fairy lights.

Underneath Merdeka Square is a shopping arcade with restaurants and a theatre where there are often performances by the **Actors' Studio** theatre group.

North of the Padang is **St Mary's Church**, built in 1894 and the first brick Anglican church in Malaysia. Like the other buildings around Merdeka Square it was designed by A C Norman but in a very different style. Its design is pure English countryside, all simplicity and stained glass. It was built at a cost of $5168, part of which was raised by public subscription. Contributors included the Kapitan China (Yap Ah Loy) and a Mr Thamboosamy Pillay who gave $50.

It is pretty enough inside with seating for about 200 people. Its stained-glass windows were installed in 1904 and remained in place until, fearful of Japanese bombs, the congregation removed them to storage in 1941. Sadly they were never found again and a new set replaced them in 1955.

> **St Mary's Church**
> ✉ Jalan Raja
> ☎ 60 3 2692 8614
> ◷ various services between 07:00 and 10:30 and at 18:00 Sun, and 19:30 Wed, Thu, Fri
> 🚍 Putra/Star line Masjid Jamek LRT
> 👤 Admission is free.

> **Independence Day**
> The best time to visit Merdeka Square is at midnight on 30/31 August, the eve of National Day when thousands of people cram into the area to celebrate the beginning of Malaysia's Independence, first declared in 1957 here in this spot which represented the core of British rule of the Malayan colony.

Below: *St Mary's Church, near Merdeka Square.*

Chinese Religion
Chinese religion is a strange and quite pragmatic mixture of several sets of beliefs. **Taoism** is an ancient almost animistic religion where ideas are personified as godlike figures. Another ancient belief is **Confucianism**, which is more a system of moral values than a set of spiritual beliefs. Most Chinese temples also have a room dedicated to the **Buddha**.

See Map B–D5 ★★★

CHINATOWN AND ITS TEMPLES

To the southeast of the Central Market lies Chinatown, where once Yap Ah Loy's empire of wooden houses stood. It is still seriously unreconstructed and chaotic, with traffic blaring its way along Jalan Cheng Lock and side streets filled with crumbling shophouses, all still in business either as coffee shops or selling dried goods or traditional medicine. Above the shops and through the open shutters can be heard the din and clatter of mah jong tables, while outside, as the day progresses, the stallholders begin to display their wares. The atmosphere reaches fever pitch when the night market begins. Here you can buy fake merchandise, from Prada handbags to Rolex watches. By sunset there are any number of streetside cafés trying to lure customers to their tables, and getting past the more determined menu bearers is an extreme sport. If you are going to eat here look for places that have local patrons.

Chinatown has three good temples to visit. The first brings back the name of Yap Ah Loy, Kapitan China, since it was he who built it in 1883. It is called the **See Yeoh Temple** and stands at the junction of Jalan Cheng Lock and Jalan Tun H S Lee. It is dedicated to Kong Seng, a tin mine tycoon murdered during the troubles of the late 19th century. You can usually see a photograph of the man himself on one of the altars.

Below: *As evening falls, the street markets of Chinatown get ready for the bustle and the crowds.*

CHINATOWN AND ITS TEMPLES

| *See* Map B–D5 | ★★★ |

At the southernmost end of Jalan Petaling is the more ornate **Chan See Shu Yuen Temple**, built in 1906 and more typical of temples of the area with an open courtyard and symmetrical buildings. Like all Chinese temples it is dedicated to several deities, including the Buddha, but its chief object of worship is Chong Wah, an emperor of the Sung Dynasty.

The most colourful and lively of the temples in Chinatown is the Hindu **Sri Mahamariamman Temple** on Jalan H S Tun Lee. The temple was built in the 1870s by Tamil immigrants who arrived to work on the railways. It was the first Hindu temple to be built in Malaysia and the cash for the project was found by a small caste of Indian people called Chettiars who were traditionally money lenders. The temple is typically south Indian with the huge ornately decorated *gopuram* or gate tower. The temple, and in particular the *gopuram*, was renovated in the 1960s when Indian sculptors were brought in to provide new figures of the deities who adorn the tower. Inside, worship is a much noisier affair than westerners are used to. Worshippers visit each of the shrines in turn offering coconuts and other gifts. In an inner room is kept the golden chariot which houses the figure of Lord Murugan and which is carried each year at Thaipusam to the **Batu Caves** (*see* page 26). When you visit the temple you must respect the feelings of those inside and leave your shoes at the entrance gate.

Above: *The five-tiered gopuram of the Sri Mahamari-amman Temple, dedicated to the deity Mariamman who protects against sickness and 'unholy incidents'.*

<u>**See Yeoh Temple**</u>
✉ 14A Lebuh Pudu
☎ 60 3 232 9593
🕐 08:00–18:00 daily
♿ Admission is free.
🚇 Putra/Star Line
Masjid Jamek LRT

<u>**Chan See Shu Yuen Temple**</u>
✉ 172 Jalan Petaling
☎ 60 3 239 6511
🕐 08:00–18:00 daily
♿ Admission is free.
🚇 Putra Line
Pasar Seni LRT

<u>**Sri Mahamariamman Temple**</u>
✉ 163 Jalan Tun H S Lee
☎ 60 3 238 3647
🕐 06:00–21:00 daily
♿ Admission is free.
🚇 Putra Line
Pasar Seni LRT

⊛ *See Map B–A5*   ★★★

Above: *A keeper prepares for another performance at the Bird Park.*

THE LAKE GARDENS

Laid out in the 1890s by Alfred Venning, British State treasurer to what was then Malaya, **Taman Tasek Perdana**, the Lake Gardens, consist of 104ha (257 acres) of sculpted parkland built around an artificial lake (Tasek Perdana). If you have children or like wildlife this is worth a repeat visit since in the grounds of the park are hibiscus gardens, a bird park, a butterfly park, an orchid garden and a deer park.

Entering the park along Jalan Parliamen, the first point of interest is the **National Monument**, designed by Felix de Weldon, the man who also created the Iwo Jima monument in Washington DC. This one commemorates those who died in World War II and the Emergency (*see* page 10). Below it is the **ASEAN Sculpture Garden** with constructions donated by many of Malaysia's neighbouring states.

Heading south along Jalan Cenderawasih brings you to the **Deer Park**, which is a pretty, enclosed area with free-ranging and quite tame deer. The animals you are most likely to spot here are mouse deer – the world's smallest hoofed creature and a native of Malaysia.

Close by is the **Butterfly Park**, another enclosed space, this one containing a rich variety of butterflies. The planting in the enclosure aims to reproduce a native rain-

---

Tai Chi
If you visit the Lake Gardens in the early morning, you'll see groups of people practising the art of Tai Chi. Perhaps there are not as many adherents as fill the parks and open spaces of Beijing and Hong Kong but it is nonetheless a fascinating sight to watch the slow and graceful synchronized movements of this age-old Taoist system of traditional callisthenics aimed at achieving a calm state of mind and physical well-being.

THE LAKE GARDENS

forest and is said to contain approximately 100 plant species and 120 species of butterfly. Some of them are bred in the park.

The park is also home to an **orchid garden**, with 800 different species, and a **hibiscus garden**. Both of these can be visited on the way to the Deer Park or the Bird Park.

The highlight of the park, well worth an hour or two, is the **Bird Park**, built in 1991 to compete with Singapore's longer established sight. It is the world's largest covered aviary, at 3.2ha (8 acres) of naturally landscaped gardens, and contains more than two thousand birds, including the world's largest pheasant, the strange native hornbills, birds of prey and many more. Some are caged but many of them roam free within the park.

West of the park is the splendid **Carcosa Seri Negara**, once the residence of the British governor and more recently converted to a posh hotel for visiting VIPs. The hotel is open to the public for afternoon tea, which is truly one of the most fun things to do in Kuala Lumpur. Sitting out on the huge veranda you can just imagine the wallahs and white-suited flunkeys of old bringing lemonade to the memsahibs in the heat of the afternoon. The hotel (*see* page 59) also has a great restaurant.

The Bird Park
✉ The Lake Gardens
☎ 2272 1010
🕐 09:00–18:30 daily
💰 RM22
🚌 Bus 22 to main entrance then park shuttle bus

The Butterfly Park
✉ The Lake Gardens
☎ 2693 4299
🕐 09:00–18:00
💰 RM5
🚌 Bus 22 then park shuttle bus

Orchid and Hibiscus Gardens
✉ The Lake Gardens
🕐 09:00–18:00
💰 Weekdays free, Sat, Sun RM1
🚌 Bus 22 then park shuttle bus
See page 43 for canoeing in the Lake Gardens.

Below: *Hibiscus flowers provide nectar for the many species of butterflies which thrive in the Butterfly Park.*

See Map B–G4/H4 ★★★

The Great Sale
Several times a year the shops around the Golden Triangle decide to have a group sale, when all kinds of things are reduced by as much as 70%. If you are here during one of these sales, it would be a good time to do your shopping.

BUKIT BINTANG AND THE GOLDEN TRIANGLE

The bustling streets around Jalan Bukit Bintang, Jalan Sultan Ismail and Jalan Imbi form what the locals refer to as the Golden Triangle – the area of KL where there must surely be a world record of some kind regarding retail outlets. Big department stores are here, as are some of the poshest hotels in KL, some great places to eat and a long strip of designer coffee shops and bars. Changkat Bukit Bintang, a turning off Jalan Bukit Bintang, has a more informal atmosphere.

Start your visit with a walk along Jalan Bukit Bintang where the pavement cafés blast out freezing air and the coffee scents the evening breezes. Here you can people-watch while drinking your flavoured skinny latte before moving on to some serious shopping in Lot 10 or Sungei Wang Plaza. In the evening, walk around to Jalan Alor where the hawker stalls are thick on the ground and it's just a matter of selecting the least frenetic place to eat. Later on there are nightclubs to visit along Jalan Sultan Ismail. It's not as cool as Bangsar but the happy hours are good value and there is often some good live music.

Below: *A part of KL's shopping frenzy: Lot 10 has brand-name outlets and the Isetan department store.*

See Map B–B6 | ★★

THE NATIONAL MUSEUM

At the southern edge of the Lake Gardens is the National Museum of Malaysia. The museum was purpose built in 1963 in Malay style with the curving roofs typical of the traditional Minankabu architecture common around Melaka. Even the outside of the museum is impressive with specially made decorative tiles showing aspects of Malaysia's history.

Above: *A popular destination at weekends, the National Museum is both instructive and entertaining.*

Entering at the back of the building you discover signs of the vanishing world of Malaysian *kampung* life, with models of activities: weaving ceremonial cloths, tending animals and crops, and fishing. There is a diorama of a customary Malay wedding with the bride and groom in traditional dress seated on thrones and the guests offering decorated eggs.

There are also displays of Peranakan life, the culture which was at its strongest in Melaka and Singapore, with Chinese-style furniture but Malay dress. Peranakan is seen at its best in Melaka but this gives an idea of the wealthy, cultured lives of these people.

Wayang kulit puppets (*see* panel, page 76) are also on display on the ground floor, showing their various designs and regions.

Upstairs is a display of traditional musical instruments (most of which you are unlikely to see played unless you happen to travel to the north of Malaysia), some wicked-looking weaponry and the inevitable collection of stuffed animals which most museums seem to collect.

> **Muzium Negara**
> ✉ Jalan Damansara
> ☎ 2282 6255
> 🖥 www.
> museum.gov.my
> 🕐 09:00–18:00 daily
> 💰 RM2

Above: *Soaring skywards, the Petronas Towers dwarf the more mundane Suria KLCC shopping and entertainment centre.*

**Petronas Towers
Viewing Gallery**
✉ KLCC
☎ 2331 1769
🖥 www.petronastwin
towers.com.my
🕐 09:00–17:00
Tues–Sun, closed Mon
and for Friday prayers
13:00–14:30;
tickets available from
the ground floor infor-
mation desk, Tower 2.
💰 Free
🚍 Putra Line KLCC LRT

Petrosains Museum
✉ Level 4, Suria Shop-
ping Centre
☎ 2331 8181
🕐 09:30–16:00 Tue,
Wed, Thu; 13:30–
16:00 Fri; 09:30–17:00
Sat, Sun, public holidays
💰 RM5
🚍 Putra Line KLCC LRT
🍴 Lots of cafés and
restaurants in Suria
KLCC.

⚙ *See* Map B–H2/G2 ★★

KLCC AND THE PETRONAS TOWERS

When the old Selangor Turf Club came up for redevelopment in the early 1990s the cash rich Malaysian government saw its opportunity to create a new city centre for KL on the 40ha (100 acres) which suddenly became available. The result is the complex consisting of the Suria shopping mall, entertainment complex, office blocks and park. At its heart are the **Petronas Towers** – 88 storeys, 421m (1483 ft), 65,000m² (78,000 sq yd) of stainless steel, 77,000m² (92,100 sq yd) of glass, US$2-billion twin towers connected by a two-storey skybridge between floors 41 and 42. It is possible to travel to the skybridge and look out over the city, but the views from the Menara KL (*see* page 34) are better.

Inside, besides the shops and cinemas, is an interactive gallery dedicated to the petroleum industry and an equally interactive dinosaur exhibition (*see* page 49). In the basement is the Petronas Concert Hall, the home of the national orchestra.

Surrounding the towers and their smaller satellites is **KLCC Park**, a welcome bit of greenery in a noisy city. Roberto Burle Marx, the designer of the park, thought to protect about 40 of the turf club's original trees so the park seems more well established than it is. It includes a jogging track, children's playground, a prayer hall, an aviary, a lake and (best seen by night) the park's dancing illuminated fountains.

☆ *See* Map A–B4   ★★

BUKIT CAHAYA SRI ALAM AGRICULTURAL PARK

For anyone visiting Malaysia a compelling topic of interest has to be the amazing flora and fauna of the country, and what better way to learn about its agriculture in particular than at this well-designed and beautiful park, 50km (31 miles) west of the city. Here 1295ha (3200 acres) of tropical rainforest has been dedicated to an educational centre aimed at the city's schoolchildren but it has a lot to offer visitors of all ages. Inside the park a shuttle bus takes visitors around the various sections of the park which include a tropical fruit garden, rice paddies, a cocoa plantation, a spice garden where you can watch the process of preparing and drying the spices, a fisheries lake where visitors can try their hand at catching dinner, an aviary, lots of flower gardens, a mushroom garden, a hydroponics centre and a village where traditional culture is on display. All of these sights are well illustrated to help the visitor understand the processes behind them.

Trekkers can follow one of the many paths laid out through the forest or you can hire bikes. There are places to find refreshments around the park and at the park headquarters.

Bukit Cahaya Sri Alam Agricultural Park
🕘 09:00–16:30 Tue–Sun
💲 RM2
🚌 Bus Intrakota 338, Cityliner 222 from Klang Bus station
🍽 Canteen and food stalls in the park (carry lots of water).

Below: *A pleasant contrast of wilderness and manicured garden, the Agricultural Park offers hours of educational activity.*

Batu Caves
🕐 08:00–19:00
💰 Free
🚌 Bus 11/69 from
Central Market; last
bus from the caves
leaves at 17:30
🍽 Indian vegetarian
food and fresh coconut
water stalls.

🌐 *See* Map A–D2	★★

THE BATU CAVES

Just 13km (8 miles) north of the city the
Batu Caves stand out against the line of
limestone hills in which they have formed.
As places of worship they are relatively
new – the caves were 'discovered' in 1881
by William Hornaby, an American explorer.
They rapidly became a quaint picnic spot
for the colonials and, during World War II,
a hideout for communist opponents of
the occupying Japanese forces. Nowadays
the caves have become a centre for the
worship of the Hindu god Murugan, with
the **Subramaniam Swamy Temple** dedicated to Murugan; a shrine to Rama, the
god who protects immigrants; a shrine to
Ganesh, the elephant-headed god; a
gallery of Indian deity figures; and vegetarian restaurants with food and drinks. The
main cave, reached after a climb of 272
steps, is illuminated by shafts of light
falling through naturally occurring holes in
the roof of the cave. The walls and ceiling
of the temple are covered in pictures illus-
trating Hindu mythology.

The Batu Caves are a very popular week-
end destination for city dwellers but the

Below: *The elabo-
rate entrance to the
Batu Caves with the
272 steps leading up
to the shrine itself.*

numbers really swell here at
the festival of Thaipusam,
when devotees walk to the
caves from the city centre,
following the chariot of
Lord Murugan (*see* page
19), many of them with
their bodies pierced by
heavy *kavadis* (steel frames
or metal skewers).

See Map B–D3 ★★

LITTLE INDIA AND MASJID INDIA

Just as Brickfields (*see* page 32) can be seen as the heart of the Tamil Hindu community, the area to the north of Chinatown, along Jalan Tunku Abdul Rahman, is identifiable as the centre of north Indian Muslim culture. Like the area around Masjid Jamek, this is one of the city's oldest settlements, originally settled by the local Malays. This is a great area for roadside food. Jalan Masjid India has a definite quality of its own, with Bollywood songs roaring out of the music shops, the streets filled with sari shops and Indian-style gold and jewellery shops, stalls offering all manner of things, and a line of Indian medicine men selling cures of all kinds. Many of the healers surround themselves with some gory-looking 'before-and-after' pictures and can be seen practising their craft on their patients right there on the street. The mosque itself, built in a distinctly Indian Muslim style, is not open to non-Muslims but you can admire it from outside. The site has been a mosque since 1863 but was largely rebuilt in 1966. The style is elaborate with Islamic domes and minarets and curved windows. Look out for Medan Bunus where there are traditional Indian flower-sellers weaving flowers into all kinds of designs. Also prevalent in the area are the Chettiars, the Indian money-lenders who originally financed much of the city and who still provide working capital for small start-up businesses here.

Above: *In this shop close to one of the Indian temples, garlands, little shrines and images of the Hindu gods are for sale.*

Pasar Malam
Little India lies to the north of Masjid Jamek and is a good place to visit at night when a *pasar malam*, or night market, takes place at Lorong Bunus. Besides the Indian-style goods on sale, there are stalls offering delicious tandoori chicken and various other Indian and Malay dishes.

Above: *Stately and impressive, the National Mosque regularly holds thousands of people at Friday prayers.*

Masjid Negara
✉ Jalan Perdana
🕐 09:00–18:00, but closed Fri 14:45–18:00 for prayer. You can borrow robes from the entranceway. Remove shoes before entering. There is a separate entrance for women.
🍴 Malay food stalls atround the mosque.
🚆 Putra Line Pasar Seni LRT

The Museum of Islamic Arts
✉ Jalan Perdana
☎ 2274 2020
🕐 Tue–Sun 10:00–18:00
💰 RM8
🍴 Café in museum
🚆 Putra Line Pasar Seni LRT

See Map B–C5 ⭐ | ★★

MASJID NEGARA AND THE ISLAMIC ARTS MUSEUM

The impressive Masjid Negara, or National Mosque, was built in 1965 and reflects a new pride in Islamic culture and design. It occupies 5ha (12 acres) filled with reflective pools and great chunks of white marble. Its centrepiece is the prayer hall, designed to hold 10,000 people and roofed by an 18-pointed star signifying the 13 states of Malaysia plus the five pillars of Islam. The mosque has a single minaret.

In keeping with the Islamic proscription on portraying figures, the decoration is abstract and geometric. Inside, the roof is decorated with texts from the Koran. The 48 smaller domes inside the compound are a copy of the style of the mosque in Mecca. Inside the mosque is the mausoleum of Tun Abdul Razak, the second prime minister of Malaysia. Non-Muslims can visit the mosque between prayers but modest dress must be worn.

West of the mosque on Jalan Lembah Perdana is the shiny new **Museum of Islamic Arts** – one of the first museums in the world to dedicate itself to the subject of Islamic art. The museum is a sight in itself before you even get to the exhibits. It has a huge open-plan room which positively glows with marble. From the top floor you can observe the handiwork of craftsmen from Uzbekistan and Iran on the inverted dome of the ceiling. Exhibits include calligraphy, ceramics and metalwork.

Masjid Negara & Kuala Lumpur Zoo

See Map A–D3   ★★

KUALA LUMPUR ZOO

The National Zoo and Aquarium is 13km (8 miles) northeast of the city centre. The zoo houses some 4000 animals belongong to 400 species of Malaysian and exotic animals, birds and reptiles in a 62ha (155-acre) fenced but open enclosure, laid out around a central lake. Be prepared for some fairly cramped conditions. While the area available to visitors is wide and shady, some of the enclosures lack shade or room for animals to stretch out. The **Tunku Abdul Rahman Aquarium**, located in a dark corner at the back of the zoo, has 80 species of marine and freshwater life.

When it was originally created, the zoo was carved out of the jungle but now the surrounding jungle is pure concrete, as the city has caught up with it. Visitors can walk the extensive grounds along shady pathways to each enclosure, or just hop on and off the shuttle bus as it tours the park.

The most stunning creatures, if not the happiest ones, are the Sumatran tigers, orang utans and gibbons – all of which are very rare outside of the region.

There are train, elephant, pony, and camel rides for children, and the zoo incorporates restaurants, picnic grounds and a boating lake.

Zoo Negara Malaysia
✉ Ulu Kelang
☎ 4108 3422
🕐 09:00–17:00 daily, 19:00–23:00 Fri–Sat
💰 RM7 (adults), RM3 (children)
🚌 Bus 17 or 170 from Lebuh Ampang in Chinatown; Shuttle bus RM1
🍽 There are cafés in the grounds.

Below: *Captive but safe from predators, this Sumatran tiger will live its life roaming around its enclosure in the National Zoo.*

See Map A–C2   ★★

THE FOREST RESEARCH INSTITUTE

Forest Research Institute of Malaysia
✉ Kepong
☎ 6279 7575
🖥 www.frim.gov.my
🕐 08:00–18:30 daily
💲 RM3
🚌 Bus 148 from Jalan Hang Kasturi, Chinatown, or KTM Kommuter train to Kepong, then a taxi.
🍽 There is a canteen on site.

Canopy Walk
🕐 Tue–Sat
💲 RM5
Advance booking is necessary:
☎ 6279 7220

The real glories of Malaysia are its pristine forests, and while a real rainforest can be visited if you have the time (*see* Taman Negara, page 80), there are nearer and cheaper alternatives. One of these is **FRIM**, the Forest Research Institute of Malaysia, where there are plenty of unspoiled forest walks in 600ha (1480 acres), only 16km (10 miles) northwest of the city.

FRIM has been around since 1926 and is a serious research station studying the environment of the rainforest, but in recent years it has turned its attention to paying customers and been revamped along jungle theme park lines. The highlight of the park, for children at least, is the jungle canopy, a 20-minute walk through the treetops with views back over the city as well as across the canopy. For the ecologically dedicated there are showcase arboretums, each containing a different type of tree: monocotyledenous species, dipterocarps, indigenous fruit trees and conifers. If you plan to wander some of the forest trails, prepare as you would for serious jungle trekking – lots of water, insect repellent, good sturdy shoes and a map of the trail you are following. If you don't have the time for a walk, at least visit the museum. It tells the story of the forest and the institute and there are exhibitions of wooden artefacts.

Below: *FRIM has indigenous trees in their natural setting providing habitats for many other forest dwellers, including epiphytes which live on the trees and capture their nutrients from the atmosphere.*

See Map A–D3   ★★

THEAN HOU TEMPLE

Built on a hilltop in Seputeh, 3km (2 miles) south of the city, the six-tiered Thean Hou Temple was officially opened in 1989. It was built by KL's Hainanese community and is dedicated to the Taoist goddess Thean Hou, the water spirit and protector of seafarers. The temple, like most other Chinese temples, contains elements of other Chinese religions, with shrines to the Buddhist goddess of mercy, Kuan Yin, and one to Confucius.

Above: *The colourful entrance to the Thean Hou Temple, its red pillars offering prosperity to all those who walk through them.*

Although modern in age the temple is built along classical lines and has several traditional features. The red pillars at the entrance to the temple denote prosperity and good fortune while the prayer hall is decorated with intricate patterns of lanterns and writhing dragons, the symbol of life.

Many Chinese choose to have their wedding here, partly for the excellent photo opportunities. The registry is inside the temple and the second floor can be hired for the reception.

Like many Chinese temples this one offers a fortune-telling service. Worshippers shake a canister of numbered sticks until one falls out and then collect the printed fortune that goes with the number.

In the garden at the back are the statues of the god of longevity, the god of wealth and the god of happiness as well as statues representing the 12 animals of the Chinese cycle of years.

Thean Hou Temple
✉ 65 Pesiaran Indah, off Jalan Syed Putra
☎ 2274 7088
🕐 09:00–18:30 daily
💰 Free
🚌 Bus 27/52 from Klang bus station.

⊗ *See* Map B–B6   ★

Above: *Still essentially Indian in nature, Brickfields may soon be just another modern suburb if the planners get their way.*

BRICKFIELDS AND THE TEMPLE OF FINE ARTS

Just 2km (1.25 miles) south of the Central Market lies Brickfields, named for the many brick kilns set up in the area at the end of the 19th century to burn bricks for the city's new buildings. The workers who settled in the brickyards and their surrounding enclaves were mostly south Indian and the area still has a strongly Tamil feel to it. Some of the older buildings from this period still remain but for a limited time only – now the new railway station has opened in the area there are plans to redevelop it. The neighbourhood is worth a visit just to catch a sense of the old KL before it goes, for the cheap and good restaurants, the mildly seedy, but completely safe, atmosphere, and for the **Temple of Fine Arts** which is a centre for Indian culture. The temple offers Indian dance and music lessons and there are regular performances of classical Indian music as well as dance dramas. The temple also has a fine vegetarian café.

Also in Brickfields is the **Maha Vahara Buddhist Temple**, the centre of Buddhist teaching and worship in Malaysia.

Temple of Fine Arts
✉ 116 Jalan Berhala, Brickfields
☎ 2274 3709
🕑 11:00–21:00
💰 Free
🍽 Vegetarian café

See Map B–A6   ★

BANGSAR

To the west of Brickfields a new and relatively unplanned part of the city has sprung up in what was once a quiet suburb. A good night market and a few restaurants with attitude began the area's transformation in the early 1990s, and now the place is the coolest spot to be, especially on a Sunday night. From early evening the streets are filled with beautiful people who go there to party all night and they have lots of places to do their partying. Go for the *pasar malam*, the excellent wetmarket which sells all kinds of food and domestic items as well as all the same old fake labels. About six city blocks makes up the area which includes Internet cafés, a useful bookshop, two hawker centres, and a continuing and varied range of innovative places to eat and drink. People who fly off to Europe on the Monday morning flight have been known to spend their last night at Bangsar, enjoying the market and partying the night away before staggering onto their plane the next morning, ready to sleep through the long flight to their destination.

Bangsar
🕐 *Pasar malam* from 17:00 on Sundays
🚌 Bus 5 from Jalan Sultan Mohammed terminus; the last bus from Bangsar leaves at 23:00.
🍽 Jalan Telawi Tiga Food Centre and outdoor stalls

Below: *All kinds of delicious items are on offer in the hawker stalls and restaurants of Bangsar.*

Above: *Taking a train from the old railway station was always more of an adventure because of the building's romantic architectural style.*

Polite Temple Behaviour
Visitors are very welcome in Hindu temples as long as they remember that this may seem colourful and outlandish to them but it is part of a sincerely held religion. Visitors should remove their shoes at the temple door and keep quietly in the background. Temple officials will explain what is going on if they are not busy.

Architecture
Stesen Keretapi Kuala Lumpur

Now decommissioned as KL's major **train station**, this 1910 building was created by that old diehard A B Hubbock, whose time in India had such an influence on his designs for the colonial government of the city. The best views of the station are from Jalan Kinabalu where you can appreciate the crazy architecture of domes, minarets and Islamic designs. Inside, the building is a typical British turn-of-the-century railway station complete with cast-iron shelters and wooden decorations.
✉ *Jalan Sultan Hishamuddin*

Bangunan KTM Berhad

Directly opposite the railway station on Jalan Cheng Lock is the slightly later (1917) **Railway Administration Building**, also a Hubbock classic. The last of Hubbock's efforts, it, along with his other works, seems to encapsulate that period in the history of this country.
✉ *Jalan Sultan Hishamuddin*

Menara Kuala Lumpur

On the top of Bukit Nanas, just north of the city centre, stands Menara Kuala Lumpur, officially opened in 1996. The 421m (1379ft) building is essentially a communications tower but it also stands as a symbol of the new wealth of the city. Designed to look like a traditional Malaysian toy, the spinning top, the tower includes offices and a shopping mall with cascading pools and geometric glass domes at the lower levels, while four lifts and a 2058-step staircase take you to a public observation platform and revolving restaurant at a height of 276m (910ft). Above that again is the antenna mast used for telecommunications and broadcasting transmissions.

✉ *Jalan Bukit Nanas*
🕐 *daily 09:00–22:00*
💰 *RM8, viewing gallery RM15*
🚇 *Monorail: Bukit Nanas*

Pak Ali's

Some 10km (6 miles) outside the city and en route to the Batu Caves is Pak Ali's house, built in the early 20th century by Haji Abbas bin Haji, the headman of Gombak village. It is typical of a Malay *kampung* built on stilts to protect the occupants from flooding and to create a cool space below the house and ventilate the inside. The house is furnished inside in a traditional manner and divided in the traditional way into five sections. It is built almost entirely from wood cut out of what was once the surrounding jungle. The woodwork is elaborately carved in the style of Sumatran architecture. It is open to the public.

✉ *10km mark along Jalan Gombak*
🕐 *daily 09:00–17:00*
💰 *RM3*
🚌 *Bus 11 from Pasar Seni*

Millionaire's Row

Starting from KLCC, Jalan Ampang grows steadily more ornate and old-fashioned as you leave town. This is the road where most of the Chinese tin millionaires chose to build their mansions alongside British colonial homes. The styles of these houses range from Art Deco to just plain over-the-top. Gradually these houses are giving way to more modern, streamlined buildings but those that survive are a grand reminder of times past. Visit the **Malaysian Tourism Centre** at number 109 where besides getting lots of tourist advice you can admire the style of the building. It was built in 1935 by Eu Tong Seng, a rubber millionaire, and occupied by the Japanese during World War II.

🚆 *Putra Line: Dang Wangi LRT*

Museums and Galleries
Royal Malaysian Police Museum

West of the Islamic Arts Museum is this little gem of a place – a museum dedicated to the history of the Malaysian police. It is full of memorabilia of the bad old days:

Private Art Galleries
If Malaysian art interests you there are many commercial galleries in the city where you can go to admire the work of local artists and perhaps buy a piece to take home:
A P Art Gallery,
⌧ Ground Floor
☎ 2274 6724
Central Market
Art Salon,
⌧ 4 JalanTelawi 2, Bangsar ☎ 2282 2601
🕘 09:00–18:30
Mon–Sat.
ArtFolio Gallery,
⌧ Floor 3, City Square, Jalan Tun Razak
☎ 2162 3339
🕘 11:00–20:00
Galeri Petronas,
⌧ Floor 3 Suria KLCC
☎ 2051 7770
🕘 10:00–20:00

Below: *The National Planetarium can provide a great day out for the kids and keep them occupied for hours.*

Japanese armoured cars, *parangs* and other weapons from the Emergency, and also old photos of the colonials.
⌧ *Jalan Perdana*
☎ *2272 5689*
🕘 *10:00–18:00 Tue–Sun*
🔔 *Free*
🚈 *Putra Line KL Sentral LRT*

The National Planetarium

Close by the National Museum is the Planetarium. Apart from a 36cm (14 in) telescope and a theatre with shows in Malay and English about the night sky, it also offers lots of information about Malaysia's own space exploration, a history

of astronomy, an IMAX theatre and a gyroscope where you can enjoy the effects of zero gravity. Also look out for the viewing gallery with excellent views over the city and the garden with replicas of ancient observatories.
⌧ *53 Jalan Perdana*
☎ *2273 4303*
🕘 *09:30–16:15 Tue–Sun*
🔔 *RM3, Space Theatre RM6*
🚈 *Putra Line KL Sentral LRT*

Numismatic Museum

This museum covers the history of exchange in Southeast Asia, from cowrie shells and rice to plastic. It has everything ever used as coinage in the area, including coins produced by the various rubber and tin companies with their own name and logo. Worth a visit if you're interested in the subject. There's a food-and-drink centre alongside it, all inside a building

worthy of note for its 1980s Islamic design.

✉ *Ground Floor, Maybank Building, Jalan Tun Perak*

☎ *2070 8833*

⏰ *daily 10:00–18:00*

💰 *Free*

🚈 *Star Line Plaza Rakyat LRT*

National Museum of History

Once part of the colonial government offices, this Moorish building was converted in the 1990s to an interesting little museum dedicated to the history of what is now Malaysia. Some very old stones and skulls are among the exhibits.

✉ *29 Jalan Rajah*

☎ *2694 4590*

⏰ *daily 09:00–18:00*

💰 *Free*

🚈 *Star/Putra Line Masjid Jamek LRT*

National Art Gallery

Set in a beautiful purpose-built gallery, the national art collection sets out to showcase Malaysian

talent and does so quite effectively.

✉ *2 Jalan Temerloh, off Jalan Tun Razak*

☎ *4025 4990*

⏰ *daily 10:00–18:00*

💰 *Free*

Museum of Aboriginal Affairs

A little way out of the city (20km, 12.5 miles) for a cursory visit, the **Orang Asli Museum** is about the best insight any visitor can hope for into these pre-industrial people and their lives. The museum showcases their habitats, the various ethnic groups within the Orang Asli, the various lifestyles they have adopted and much more.

Above: *A welcome in two languages greets visitors to the Orang Asli Museum, one of the area's more informative and lively museums.*

Religion of the Orang Asli

The Orang Asli are chiefly animists, that is they believe that the naturally occurring elements of the world are imbued with a spirit. In the **Museum of Aboriginal Affairs** are displays on the religion of the local Orang Asli people who practise ancestor worship. Displays include a series of carved wooden heads with fierce expressions, representing the deity Moyang.

Above: *Kanching Recreational Forest is just a bus ride away from the city centre.*

Opposite: *This orchid flourishes in the managed landscapes of the university's Botanic Gardens.*

✉ *Gombak Road*
☎ *6182 2122*
🕐 *09:00–17:00 Sat–Thu*
💰 *Free*
🚌 *Bus 174 from Lebuh Ampang. Ask the driver to let you off at the museum.*

Places of Worship
Sri Ganesar Temple

This is a major Hindu place of worship in Kuala Lumpur and is dedicated to the elephant-headed god Ganesh. The temple was founded in 1897 in the backyard of an English official's house. When the official threatened to destroy the shrine his gardener had built his limbs became paralysed. Ganesh appeared to the gardener in a dream and told him to smear some ashes on his employer's limbs. The official, of course, recovered and was so grateful that he paid for a proper temple. Just as interesting as the temple are its surroundings, with garland-makers, incense-sellers, and stalls selling Indian sweets.

✉ *13 Jalan Pudu Lama*
☎ *2222 4242*
🕐 *daily 08:00–18:00*
💰 *Free*
🚌 *Star Line Plaza Rakyat LRT*

Green Spaces
Kanching Recreational Forest

Some 10km (6 miles) further up the road from the Batu Caves, this would make an interesting extension of a day trip. The main attraction is an uphill walk past a waterfall. You will need sturdy footwear

– sandals will be found wanting – and bring plenty of water. There are resting places on the walk where a picnic could be enjoyed, though there is a food stall near the main entrance. If possible, try to avoid weekends because the place can easily become too full.

🚌 *Bus 66, 72, 83 from Pudu Raya bus station. Buses leave on the hour and the last bus back to KL departs at 20:00. Buy your return ticket at the Forest Office.*
☎ *6091 6131*
🕐 *08:00–20:30*
💰 *Free*

Botanic Gardens

Rimba Ilmu, the 40ha (100-acre) botanic gardens were established in 1974 by the University of Malaysia's Botany Department for ecological and educational purposes but are worth a visit for their excellent planting and for a sight of some rare tropical plants and birds. There are waste recycling projects, studies of useful tropical plants, and a rainforest exhibition. On the first Saturday of each month there is a guided tour of the gardens.

✉ *University of Malaysia, Lembah Pantai*
☎ *7959 4690*
🕐 *Mon–Fri 08:45–15:30, Sat 08:45–23:30*
💰 *Free; guided tour at 09:00 on 1st Sat of month costs RM4.*

Lake Titiwangsa

A popular recreational park situated 3km

Hinduism

Hinduism has been practised in Malaysia for around 1500 years but was largely replaced by Islam which was brought to the peninsula by traders and gradually absorbed other religions. Hinduism worships a pantheon of gods, all of whom are aspects of a single deity. The three chief aspects are personified by **Brahma** (the Creator), **Vishnu** (the Preserved) and **Shiva** (the Destroyer). The caste system, which is still an important part of Hindu culture in other countries, has never been important in Malaysia since the thousands of Indian labourers who re-established Hinduism in Malaysia in the 19th century were chiefly of low caste origin.

Menara Kuala Lumpur: Saving a Tree
Unusually for a country with a fairly gung-ho attitude to cutting down trees, some considerable expense went into saving one particular tree on Bukit Nanas when Menara Kuala Lumpur (*see* page 34) entered its final planning stages. The original site for the tower rested on a spot occupied by a 100-year-old Jelutong tree (*Dyera costulata*) and in order to preserve the tree the whole project was shifted slightly to one side. The tree was shored up and protected at a total cost of RM430,00.

(2 miles) north of the city, Lake Titiwangsa lies in 46ha (114 acres) of parkland with picnic areas, jogging tracks, horse riding facilities, and a gym with courts for tennis, squash, volleyball and table tennis. The lake offers boat hire and a dancing fountain. Though very popular with the locals, this remains a pleasant green space with some excellent hawker stalls.

✉ *Jalan Kuantan*
🚌 *Bus 172 from Lebuh Ampang*
🛶 *Boat hire RM5 (see page 43)*

Bukit Nanas Recreational Park
Surrounding the Menara Kuala Lumpur is the tiny but well-preserved little piece of rainforest called Bukit Nanas. At only 10.5ha (26 acres), it still represents the largest forested area in the city. On the 45-minute tour, visitors are introduced to the rubber tree and some of the flora and fauna of Malaysia.

✉ *Jalan Punchak, off Jalan P. Ramlee*
☎ *2034 2609*
🕐 *08:00–18:00*
🚌 *Monorail: Bukit Nanas*

Right: *It is not often you find yourself alone in the heart of the city but Lake Titiwangsa can be a good place to find a bit of peace and solitude.*

Left: *There's quite a contrast between the solitude of Titiwangsa lake and the collective fun and games of the Sunway Lagoon.*

ACTIVITIES
Sport and Recreation
Golf

Golf is an upwardly mobile sport in Malaysia, with courses springing up faster than mushrooms in horse manure. In the city itself there are several golf courses which are open to non-members. **Kuala Lumpur Golf and Country Club** has two courses of 9 holes and 18 holes.

Swimming and Water Sports

All the five-star hotels in KL have pools for their guests. The **Kompleks Renang Kuala Lumpur** has an Olympic-sized pool (🛢 RM1). There are also public swimming pools at **Bangsar Sports Complex, Chin Woo Stadium**, and a water theme park at **Sunway Lagoon** (*see* page 49).

Racquet Sports

There are lots of public sports centres in the city, which offer courts for **tennis, badminton, squash, volleyball** and more. They are generally open from 08:00–23:00 (*see* panel, this page).

Golf
Kuala Lumpur Golf and Country Club,
✉ 10 Jalan 1/70D, off Jalan Bukit Kiara
☎ 253 1111
🕐 06:00–24:00 daily
🛢 Green fees for non-members from RM120.

Swimming
Bangsar Sports Complex,
✉ Jalan Terasek 3
☎ 2284 6065
Chin Woo Stadium,
✉ off Jalan Hang Jebat
☎ 232 4602
Kompleks Renang,
✉ Jalan Tentram, Bandar Tun Razak
☎ 2931 6353

Racquet Sports
Kampung Datuk Keramat,
☎ 2456 4853
🕐 08:00–23:00 daily
Taman Tasik Titiwangsa,
☎ 2423 9558
🕐 08:00–23:00 daily
Bandar Tun Razak Sports Complex,
☎ 8930 8935
🕐 08:00–23:00 daily

Above: *Imagine running all the way to the top! The Menara Kuala Lumpur is the location for the city's annual towerthon.*

Horse Riding
STC Equestrian and Sports Centre,
✉ Jalan Kuda Emas, off Jalan Sungei Besi
☎ 9050 2346
🕐 07:15–10:15 Tue–Sun

Martial Arts
Persatuan Seni Silat Gayung Malaysia,
✉ Jalan Penerbitan, Universiti Malaya
☎ 987 5051
Persatuan Seni Silat Sendeng,
✉ 34-3G, Jln AU 1A/4A, Taman Keramat Permai, Sekolah Menengah Wangsa Maju R1-Seksyen 1, Wangsa Maju
☎ 4142 7201

Bowling

Indoor tenpin bowling is a popular sport. City-centre venues include: **Sports Toto Bowling** (✉ 4.1, Plaza Berjaya 12, Jalan Imbi, Kuala Lumpur, 🕐 10:00–01:00); **Federal Bowl** (✉ Federal Hotel, 35 Jalan Bukit Bintang, Kuala Lumpur, ☎ 2148 9166, 🕐 10:00–24:00). *See* panel for other bowling venues.

Horse Riding

There are several places around the city where horse riding is possible. The **STC Equestrian and Sports Centre** is an Olympic-sized venue for **polo** and **show jumping** but also offers pleasure riding without membership fees. Coaches are available for new riders. Located near the KL-Seremban expressway, it is only about 15 minutes' drive from the city centre.

Local Sports

Malaysia has its own form of martial arts called *Seni Silat Melayu*, an ancient form of fighting which descends from the Malay Royal households of the 11th century. It is a close combat form of fighting and uses weapons such as the *kris*, a Malay dagger, scarves and sticks. It is an inclusive style of fighting using punching, kicking, throws, pressure points and more. Like other martial arts the discipline involves character building as much as physical training and is led by a guru. The syllabus includes art, music and dance. Practitioners consider it to be both devastating as a form of combat and beautiful as an art. Watch it in displays organized by the tourist board, or call up one of the clubs to join in a practice session. Most charge by the month for tuition but rates are low and you might enjoy it.

The Towerthon

Menara Kuala Lumpur, the world's fourth tallest telecommunication tower, is the venue for this race. The increasingly popular sport of staircase running attracts global participants to Asia's highest run. The race begins at the bottom of Bukit Nanas and involves a steep 800m (875yd) uphill dash to the base of the tower. The runners then negotiate the 2058 steps of the tower itself. Usually held in May, the people to contact if you are interested in joining in are the **Malaysian Tourism Office** (☎ 2164 3929 for more information).

Canoeing

There are two easy-to-reach places in Kuala Lumpur where canoes are available for hire on a boating lake. One is Lake Titiwangsa (*see* page 40) and canoes are available from 10:30–17:00 on weekdays and from 08:30–18:00 on weekends and public holidays. The other place to hire canoes is the Lake Gardens (*see* pages 20–21), with the same hours as Lake Titiwangsa.

Spectator Sports

Horse Racing

Kuala Lumpur has a beautiful new turf club on the KL-Seremban highway with six meetings a year. There is seating for 25,000, plus loads of monitors showing home races as well as others from around the state and abroad.

Bowling
Bangsar Bowl,
✉ Bangsar Shopping Centre, 285 Jalan Maarof, 4/F Bukit Bandarya Bangsar
☎ 2094 3498
Cosmic Bowl,
✉ In the same shopping centre as Bangsar Bowl.
☎ 9282 2228

Horse Racing
Selangor Turf Club,
✉ Jalan Kuda Emas, off Jalan Sungei Besi
☎ 8958 3888

Below: *The Malaysia Tourism Centre, where helpful and informative staff wait to assist you.*

ACTIVITIES

Motor Racing

The **Sepang Circuit**, rated as one of the best in the world, is the venue for the annual Malaysian Grand Prix.

Football, Cricket, Rugby and Hockey

There are matches of one kind or another on the **Padang** most weekends. Professional football is played at **Merdeka Stadium** in Kuala Lumpur and also at the **Shah Alam Stadium** at Shah Alam.

Kuala Lumpur International Tower Jump

Occurring usually once a year at the beginning of March, 50 or more skydivers from around the world jump from around the 73rd floor of the Petronas Towers. This is BASE jumping, using a parachute to jump from fixed objects, and the term is an acronym that stands for the four categories of objects from which jumps are made: Building, Antenna, Span, Earth, with divers freefalling for three seconds to be clear of the tower before releasing their chutes. The displays usually include other aerobatics – radio-controlled aircraft, aeronautical displays by light aircraft, and helicopter tricks. For more information, *see*  www.kltowerjump.com

Kuala Lumpur Marathon

There are two big events to look out for in the city, whether you want to watch others suffering from heat exhaustion or take part in it yourself. They are the **Kuala Lumpur International Marathon** (

Polo
First brought to the country by the British, polo has lingered on in the armed forces. Malaysia has nine affiliated clubs and there are occasionally matches close to the city.

Royal Malaysian Polo Association
✉ Jalan Ampang Hilir
☎ 4256 4531

Sepang Circuit
☎ 8526 2040
✆ kumar@
malaysiangp.com.my

Merdeka Stadium
✉ Jalan Stadium, off
Jalan Hang Jebat
☎ 2132 6323

Shah Alam Stadium
✉ Shah Alam
☎ 5519 7766

Below: *The Padang, with the Royal Selangor Club in the background, where cricket is played amid an imperial-era landscape.*

www.klmarathon.gov.my), which has been run for the past 15 years, and the **Malay Mail Big Walk** (⌨ www.mmail.com.my. bigwalk). The marathon is an international one and is open to all. It is held around February–March in conjunction with the celebration of Kuala Lumpur City Day. The race starts and finishes at Independence Square.

Alternative KL

Unlike its intolerant near neighbour Singapore, and out of keeping with the official Malaysian government line which is positively gay unfriendly, Kuala Lumpur, like most cosmopolitan cities, is a relatively tolerant place. Bear in mind though that under Shariah law Muslim gays and lesbians can expect severe punishment if they are arrested. A good website for advice and contacts is: ⌨ www.utopia-asia.com

Above: *The Petronas Towers with the sky-bridge looking very flimsy from this angle. Skydivers take off from the 73rd floor on Federal Territory Day.*

Besides the many places to see and be seen alongside the heterosexual community there are a number of dedicated and gay-friendly bars and clubs. The most popular and most overt venue is **Liquid**, ✉ 2-04 Central Market Annexe, ☎ 2078 5909, ⌨ www.liquidbar.com.my with lots of loud dance music and a pretty terrace overlooking the city. The first Thursday of the month is open-mike night for lesbians. Older than Liquid is **Blue Boy**, ✉ 50 Jalan Sultan Ismail, where there are as many expats and tourists as locals but which can get very crowded. **Café Café**, ✉ 175 Jalan Maharajalela, ☎ 2141 8141, is very international in style and cuisine. **Velvet**, ✉ G-02 Central Plaza, is more of a venue for locals but with a relaxed and friendly atmosphere. Lastly you might like

Some more venues
My Place/Unclub,
✉ 44 Jln Pudu Lama
☎ 2078 9248
Delawi,
✉ Jln Telawi 2 Bangsar
Mixed bar with good house music.
Café Silhouette,
✉ 19A-LGF-12 UOA Centre (Jln Pinang and Jln Perak)
Drag show nightly.

Above: *Walking the city is best at night when the food stalls spill out over the street, the traffic slows down to a dull roar and the people are less hurried and more inclined to chat.*

City Centre Sights

If you enjoy walking, a good way to check out the major sights in the city is to start at Masjid Jamek, head south along Jalan Benteng, past some of KL's oldest brick buildings to the Central Market. From there you can head eastwards into Jalan Cheng Lock to admire the crumbling shophouses and temples of Chinatown. Back to Central Market and along Lebuh Pasar Besar brings you to Merdeka Square and the sights around it.

---

to look in at **La Queen Club**, ⊠ 5 Jalan P. Ramlee, ☎ 017 325 9985, on a Saturday or Friday night. **Shook**! at ⊠ B/F Starhill Shopping Complex, Jalan Bukit Bintang, is a gay-and-lesbian-friendly place with a relaxed atmosphere but slightly higher than average prices and a smart casual dress code.

Walking the City

Walking is not a particularly leisurely activity in Kuala Lumpur, where the traffic seems manic and the pedestrian crossings are thin on the ground. Also, pavements are often taken up by herds of parked motorcycles, and the heat and humidity make every café you pass seem too alluring to avoid slipping into. Having said that, there are some interesting places to walk around, perhaps starting late in the afternoon so that you get the benefit of the cool of the evening or one of the city's soothing passing showers.

A Walk Around Kampung Bahru

The district of Kampung Bahru north of the city centre is one of the oldest remaining Malay settlements in the city, probably established at the turn of the 20th century. This is a good place to visit on Saturday evening during Ramadan when the food stalls come out at dusk and people stroll out into the streets. Head up **Jalan Tuanku Abdul Rahman** (*see* Map B–D2), itself an interesting walk for the lovely old Coliseum café at the start of the road, as well as the fascinating collection of shops along the city's longest shopping street. But if you prefer take the Putra Line to interesting **Chow Kit** (Map B–E1), with its flourishing wet-market and stalls selling second-hand goods, and walk eastwards towards **Jalan Rajah Alang** where this walk begins.

By early evening this street is busy with food stalls, while further along there is a hawker centre with lots of Malay food stalls from which to choose your evening meal. As you approach the small river **Sungei Bunus**, look out for the **Sikh temple**, at number 10 on the left. The temple is pre-WWII, built in red brick like many of the old shophouses constructed around that time.

Further along the road you come to **Kampung Bahru Mosque**, a 1924 concrete building which is in keeping with the rustic atmosphere of the area. Umbrella-shaped domes and arched windows give it a Middle Eastern feel. Beyond the mosque is the original **domestic architecture** of the area: elevated houses with long verandas for maximum ventilation. At the end of the road is a Sunday **market** (Map B–F1) that starts on Saturday night, with lots of local food and atmosphere, some good local handicraft shops and stalls selling batik (*see* panel, page 13) and *songket* (a Malaysian woven fabric embellished with gold thread).

To return, make your way south to the Kampung Bahru Putra LRT station (Map B–F2).

> **A Walk Around Kampung Bahru**
> **Location:** Map B–E1
> **Distance:** about 4km (2½ miles), or just 2km (1¼ miles) if you choose to take the LRT to Chow Kit)
> **Duration:** 2–3 hours
> **Start:** Jalan Rajah Alang
> **Finish:** Jalan Rajah Alang

Below: *The traditional Malay dress and headdress are commonly seen all over the city.*

Tour Organizers
Angel Tours:
✉ 27th Floor, Central Plaza, 34 Jalan Sultan Ismail
☎ 2148 8288
Ping Anchorage:
☎ 4280 8030
🖥 www.pingachorage.com.my
Budget Tours:
go to 🖥 www.thebackpacker.net and click on Kuala Lumpur.

MATIC (Malaysian Tourist Information Complex)
✉ 109 Jalan Ampang
☎ 2164 3929
🕘 09:00–18:00

Organized Tours

The tourist office or your hotel often has leaflets describing walking tours of the city organized around the chief sights or points of architectural interest. There are some excellent tour operators in the city who can organize interesting tours of the local area or further afield, and also special interest tours. Most hotels have in-house operators but these are not necessarily the cheapest. Several operators are based in the **Tourist Office** in **Jalan Ampang** and this might be the easiest way to get to some of the more difficult places such as Taman Negara or some of the off-shore islands where there are opportunities for scuba diving.

Fun for Children

There are several things in Kuala Lumpur that are of interest to children. The **Lake Gardens** (*see* page 20) can hold a child's attention for an entire day, while the

Right: *Who can resist the doe eyes and furry antlers of this resident of the deer park in the Lake Gardens?*

Planetarium (*see* page 36) and the **National Museum** (*see* page 23) also have sections dedicated to children. The **zoo** (*see* page 29), the **Agricultural Park** (*see* page 25), the **Batu Caves** (*see* page 26), the views from the tall buildings,

poking around the shops in **Central Market** (*see* page 14), looking for computer games they don't have in the shopping malls – all these are good fun, as are the many **cinemas** around town. Besides these, there are some places that will appeal to the children in all of us.

A decade or so ago, **Sunway Lagoon** was an abandoned open-cast tin mine but its 324ha (800 acres) have been converted into a vast and, on weekends, overwhelming **theme park**. The first stage of the day's fun is at the **Water Park**, which has a surf pool, among others. After that an open-air escalator takes you to the **Adventure Park**, with seven stomach-churning rides and an indoor games arcade. If that isn't enough there is another set of rides, this time based on the **Wild West**. There is an equally vast **shopping complex** and several food courts to choose from.

Close but safe encounters with sharks at Aquaria will attract children of all ages, especially if you time your visit to take in one of the daily feeding sessions. If possible, avoid the Saturday sessions, because they are always very popular and young children will struggle to enjoy a clear view.

Above: *Making a change from the sultry temperatures of the outside is the ice-skating rink at Sunway Lagoon.*

Sunway Lagoon
✉ 3 Jalan PJS, Bandar Sunway, Petaling Jaya
☎ 5635 8000
🖥 www.sunway.com.my
🕐 11:00–18:00 Mon, Wed–Fri; 10:00–18:00 weekends and public holidays
🚆 KTM Kommuter train to Subang Jaya, then a taxi

Aquaria
✉ Concourse Level, KLCC, Jalan Ampang
☎ 2333 1888
🖥 www.klaquaria.com
🕐 11:00–20:00. Daily feeding sessions: 11:00, 12:00, 14:30 and 15:00. Shark feeding sessions at 15:00 Mon, Wed, Sat.
🚆 Putra Line KLCC

Above: *Floor upon floor of designer shops, food halls and refreshing air conditioning brings the crowds to Suria KLCC every day.*

Airport Shopping

There are plenty of shops, and signs about tax-free goods abound, but there are few bargains to be had, especially when it comes to electrical or audiovisual goods and brand-name items. At the same time, though, you need to get rid of that foreign currency which will soon be useless, and there are temptations in the way of gourmet chocolates, liquor and perfumes.

✉ KL International Airport

☎ 8777 8888

Shopping Malls

BB Plaza

Audiovisual equipment, watches, footwear, leather goods, jewellery and the like. The Metrojaya department store is here, a middle-of-the-road general store.

✉ 111 Jalan Bukit Bintang

☎ 2148 7411

Imbi Plaza

Computer hardware and software. There are bargains if you know what you're looking for. International warranties are not automatically given and, while many goods are marked up at fixed prices, some negotiating skills might be useful.

✉ Jalan Imbi

☎ 2144 9988

KL Plaza

Planet Hollywood, Tower Records, accessory shops, jewellers and boutiques.

✉ 79 Jalan Bukit Bintang

☎ 2141 7288

Lot 10 Shopping Centre

A good selection of up-market shops and designer labels. The supermarket is the Japanese Isetan, and there is a Manchester United shop near the main entrance.

✉ 50 Jalan Sultan Ismail

☎ 2141 0500

Star Hill Shopping Centre

Vuitton, Gucci, Dior – this is the epicentre for designer boutiques. There are no hordes of manic shoppers, and an air of affluence abides. Worth a gander if not a purchase, and there is always Shook! (*see* pages 46 and 62) downstairs.

✉ 181 Jalan Bukit Bintang

☎ 2148 1000

Sungei Wang Plaza

Popular and crowded. Beauty salons, amusement centres, restaurants, a department store, and outlets selling electrical/electronic goods, photography, footwear, clothes, jewellery and luggage. An overhead bridge links this mall with Lot 10 Shopping Centre.

✉ Jalan Bukit Bintang
☎ 2148 6109
💻 www.sungeiwang.com

Suria KLCC Shopping Centre

Not to be missed if you want more than a souvenir and a copy watch. Sells everything from clothes and footwear to quality arts and crafts. There's also a food centre (see page 65) and cinema.

✉ Jalan Ampang
☎ 2382 3326
💻 www.suriaklcc.com.my

Street Markets
Central Market

Once a fresh produce market, it now sells arts and crafts, clothes and souvenirs. There is a jade jewellery outlet where hard bargaining should save you half the price.
🕓 daily 10:00–22:00

Chow Kit Market

Fun market for locals and out-of-towners, with everything from clothes and footwear to fruit and vegetables.
🕓 daily 09:00 to around 17:00

Petaling Street

This is a covered, pedestrianized section of street packed with stalls selling mostly identical goods: fake designer-label clothing, bags and watches, DVDs and footwear. A shopping experience!
🕓 daily 19:00–21:30

Jalan Tuanku Abdul Rahman

Better for its atmosphere at night than for the quality of the inexpensive clothing being sold. The Sogo department store on Jalan TAR is a better bet for shopping.
🕓 daily 09:00–21:00

Mid Valley Megamall

This really is a mega-mall, one of the largest shopping, dining and entertainment centres in Southeast Asia, with over 300 speciality stores, four department stores as the 'anchor tenants', 70 places to eat and drink, and an array of cinemas. It is intensely busy at weekends.

✉ Mid Valley
☎ 2938 3333
💻 www.midvalley.com.my

Bargaining

For the westerner, bargaining is a skill that is not often practised in a world of shrink-wrapped, computer-checked shopping malls. However, in Kuala Lumpur (especially, but not only, in the markets) bargaining is de rigueur. If it is something expensive, know the price in your own country or, failing that, go to a fixed-price department store and get a price. Then you know where you can start from. If it's a small item on a market stall, just wade in with a figure far below what you're being asked. If you've bid too low they'll stop bargaining with you.

Arts and Crafts

Arch
Fine affordable wood
carvings and framed
craft work reflecting
Malaysian culture.
✉ *61 Jalan Bukit
Bintang* ☎ *2141 5616;*
✉ *Lot 307, Level 3,
Suria KLCC* ☎ *2382
0489* 🖥 *www.
archcollection.com*

Mombai Touch
Baskets, wall hangings,
photo frames, etc. from
India, East Malaysia,
Thailand and Indonesia.
✉ *KB1, Ground Floor,
Central Market*
☎ *2273 7619*

Warison Craft
Masks, wall hangings,
wooden statues and
shadow puppets.
✉ *14–16 Lorong
Melayu, Jalan Hang
Kasturi*
☎ *017 385 7128*

Petronas Towers
Gift Shop
A good selection of
items, all relating to
the Twin Towers, in a
variety of formats:
metal, pewter, cloth,
posters, jigsaws etc.

Great for souvenirs and
affordable presents.
✉ *Concourse Level,
Petronas Towers,
KLCC, Jalan Ampang*
☎ *2231 1744*

KL Arts & Crafts
An alternative to Suria
KLCC for Royal
Selangor pewter, and
at fixed prices.
✉ *G18 Central Market,
Jalan Hang Kasturi*
☎ *2274 6686* 🖥 *www.
royalselangor.com*

Native Galaxy
Goods from India,
Burma, Sarawak and
Sabah. Buddhas, masks,
wooden statues, bronze
items and gifts. No
fixed prices so be pre-
pared to bargain.
✉ *Ground Floor,
Wisma 2000, 10-12
Jalan Hang Lekir*
☎ *2070 4567*
🖥 *www.aseancraft.com*

Pucuk Rebung
An art gallery and
shop, about 20% of
what you see are
museum pieces for
display only. This still
leaves a lot of textiles,
paintings, fashion

accessories, jewellery
and other fine art and
craft items for sale.
✉ *Level 3, Suria KLCC*
☎ *2382 0769,* 🖥 *www.
pucukrebung.com*

Clothing, Fabrics and Footwear

Mng
Fashionable, sophistic-
ated clothes all from
Barcelona. Also has an
outlet in Isetan depart-
ment store in Lot 10.
✉ *C46, Concourse
Level, Suria KLCC*
☎ *2163 9818*

Izzue
Easy to find, being
located next to Planet
Hollywood, with
clothes for men and
women; cool but
expensive and defi-
nitely for the young,
or the young at heart.
✉ *180 Jalan Bukit
Bintang (Bintang Walk)*
☎ *2144 7878*
🖥 *www.izzue.com*

Jim Thomson
Top quality silk from
Thailand in the form of
soft furnishings, cloth-
ing and accessories.

✉ *Level 1, F17, Starhill Centre*
☎ *2141 8689*

Nose

Stylish women's shoes – four different outlets across the city. For less expensive footwear, there is a Bata shoe shop next door to the Suria KLCC store. In the Sungei Wang Plaza, where Nose also have an outlet, there are a lot of shoe shops.
✉ *Level 2, Suria KLCC; 1st Floor, Lot 10; Concourse Floor, Sungei Wang Plaza; Mid Valley Megamall*
☎ *2382 0278; 2142 6613; 2144 7168; 2284 9778*

Yan's Collection

Specialist Muslim-style designer garments. For Western women, the stock in such shops tends to be restricted to small sizes but Yan's Collection has a number of big sizes as well.
✉ *204, 2nd Floor, Suria KLCC*
☎ *2382 0283*

Bookshops
Kinokuniya

One of the largest bookshops in KL, part of Isetan department store. Has English literature, travel, history, art and design shelves.
✉ *Level 4, Suria KLCC*
☎ *2164 8133*

MPH Bookstore

Conveniently located; magazines, maps, travel books and contemporary bestsellers.
✉ *Ground Floor, BB Plaza, Jalan Bukit Bintang,* ☎ *2142 8231*

Skoob

Probably the best second-hand bookshop in KL and, given the high cost of books in Malaysia, an excellent place to find a book for the flight home.
✉ *88 Jalan Padang Belia, Brickfields*
☎ *2272 2731*

Above: *An excellent memento of your trip to Malaysia is a painting by a local artist. In some places you can even watch your painting take shape.*

Specialty Shops
Pewterware is a Malaysian speciality and **Royal Selangor** (✉ Lot 118, Level 1, Ramlee Mall, ☎ 2382 0240, 🖥 www.royalselangor.com) has a large collection of picture frames, flower vases, decanters, clocks, mirrors, tea canisters, tea sets, chess boards, and items suitable for children, all made out of 97% Malaysian tin and a small amount of antimony and copper. **Tea pots** and **tea sets** from the Orient could make a delightful gift or something to show off at home. Try the **Cha-No-Yu** (🕑 daily 10:00–21:00, ✉ 9 Jalan Balai Polis, ☎ 2026 7599, 🖥 www.chanoyu.com.my).

Above: The Marriot or the Westin? You are spoiled for choice in KL, with room rates that cities in the west can't compete with.

WHERE TO STAY

Kuala Lumpur has hotels and hostels to suit all budgets and there should not be a problem securing the kind of accommodation you want.

Chinatown is your likely destination if you're seeking budget accommodation, although there are also some decent mid-range hotels in this area that are well worth considering. Chinatown is the best area for atmosphere, street life and general sightseeing and there is a lot to be said for staying in this neighbourhood. For a wider choice of mid-range places and a very healthy smattering of luxury hotels, or if being close to the city's shopping and entertainment hub is important to you, the **Golden Triangle** is the obvious choice. The **KLCC** shopping mall, under the Petronas Towers, has the Mandarin Oriental as well as the **Nikko** and there are two more luxury hotels at the top end of **Jalan Putra**.

Room rates nearly always refer to the room, whether one or two people are occupying it, although sometimes it is possible to negotiate a cheaper rate for single occupancy. Room rates are often flexible and discounts off the rack rate are regularly available when demand is low. It is common practice to ask to see a room before booking it and it is sometimes possible to negotiate a slightly better deal.

Accommodation Online
Hotel websites are always worth checking for special deals and promotions, and there are a number of websites that often offer good room rates for hotels in the mid-range and luxury categories. For example:
⌨ www.bookings-asia.com, ⌨ www.asianhotels.com, ⌨ www.asia-hotels.com and, a travel portal for the region with lots of general information, ⌨ www.regit.com.

Golden Triangle

• *LUXURY*

JW Marriott

(Map B–H4)

Prestigious, 29-storey hotel with 560 rooms in the heart of the Golden Triangle. This hotel has top-notch leisure facilities, half a dozen places to enjoy a meal or a drink on the premises and an array of chic shops in the adjoining Star Hill shopping mall.

✉ *183 Jalan Bukit Bintang*

☎ *2715 9000*

📞 *2715 7000*

🖥 *www.marriott.com*

Regent (Map B–G4)

A long-time favourite, with an air of studied calmness, plus the creature comforts of a superb pool, top-of-the-range restaurants and high standards of service.

✉ *160 Jalan Bukit Bintang*

☎ *2141 8000*

📞 *2142 1441*

🖥 *www. regenthotels.com*

Berjaya Times Square Hotel & Convention Centre

(Map B–G5)

Apartments rather than hotel rooms, with kitchenettes, huge TVs, plasma screens in some, internet access. Gym and swimming pool. Expensive.

✉ *1 Jalan Imbi*

☎ *2117 8000*

📞 *2143 3352*

🖥 *www. berjayaresorts.com*

Istana (Map B–G3)

The impressive Istana (Malay for palace) is handily close to the Raja Chulan Monorail station. Large rooms with all the facilities; two mini gardens add to the charm, and there are good Italian, Chinese and Japanese restaurants.

✉ *73 Jalan Raja Chulan*

☎ *2141 9988*

📞 *2144 0111*

🖥 *www. hotelistana.com.my*

Hotel Equatorial

(Map B–G3)

A five-star hotel with modern bedrooms, popular with business travellers. With its first-rate facilities and restaurants, the hotel has consistently maintained its good name for a number of years.

✉ *Jalan Sultan Ismail*

☎ *2161 7777*

📞 *2161 9020*

🖥 *www. Equatorial.com*

• *MID-RANGE*

Bintang Warisan

(Map B–F5)

The most attractive of the mid-range hotels along this end of Jalan Bukit Bintang, with a décor – and a Heritage Coffeehouse – that aims to evoke the old-world KL. Good facilities, breakfast included. Worth considering when the room rates are discounted.

✉ *68 Jalan Bukit Bintang*

☎ *2148 8111*

📞 *2148 2333*

🖥 *www. bintangwarisan.com*

The Malaysia Hotel

(Map B–G5)

Looking a little tired,

but very centrally located and has all the basics. The rack rates are not competitive, but when discounted they come close to the top of the budget price range.

✉ 67 Jalan Bukit Bintang
☎ 2142 8033
📞 2142 8579

Hotel Agora
(Map B–G4)
Has an ancient Greek theme of sorts: the name, the look of the building, the pillars on the exterior. The deluxe rooms are best; prices may be negotiable.

✉ 110 Jalan Bukit Bintang
☎ 2142 8133
📞 2142 7815
💻 www.agorahotel.com.my

Radius International (Map B–G4)
Previously called the Park Inn International, this is a good-value, comfortable hotel in the heart of the city. The neighbouring streets

are vibrant at night. Breakfast is included and good deals may be available through their website.

✉ 51A Jalan Chankat Bukit Bintang
☎ 2715 3888
📞 2715 1888
💻 www.radius-international.com

The Lodge Hotel
(Map B–G3)
Looking a little out of place among the plush five-star hotels, The Lodge is holding its own. It has a small pool and generously sized rooms; the rates reflect the modesty of a mid-range hotel in a pricey neighbourhood.

✉ 2 Jalan Tengah
☎ 2142 0122
📞 2142 0122

Hotel Putra
(Map B–G4)
Room rates just bring the Putra into the mid-range category and the single rooms are budget price, making this one of the cheapest hotels on Jalan Bukit Bintang

and a stone's throw from all the consumer action.

✉ 72 Jalan Bukit Bintang
☎ 2141 9228
📞 2142 9678

Chinatown
• *MID-RANGE*
Ancasa Hotel
(Map B–D4)
The Ancasa is the best mid-range hotel in KL. Excellent location, next to the bus station and the Star Plaza Rakyat LRT station, and a level of service and range of facilities that match more expensive hotels, including 24-hour reception. A huge lobby, good bedroom facilities, a bar and restaurant, and breakfast is included in the price.

✉ Jalan Tun Tan Cheng Lock
☎ 2026 6060
📞 2026 8233
💻 www.vdaancasa.net

Hotel Malaya
(Map B–D5)
A well-run hotel in the heart of Chinatown.

WHERE TO STAY

Over 200 standard or superior air-conditioned rooms with telephone, TV, hair dryer, fridge and tea/coffee-making facility, and a pleasant breakfast room.
✉ Jalan Hang Lekir
☎ 2072 7722
✆ 2070 0980
🖥 www.hotelmalaya.com.my

Mandarin Pacific

(Map B–D5)
Not to be confused with the five-star Mandarin Oriental, this hotel is in the heart of Chinatown. Rooms are cheaper than many other mid-range hotels in this area but they still have air conditioning, a kettle, safe deposit and fridge. There is a laundry service, a coffee shop, and a travel agents on the well-run premises.
✉ 2-8 Jalan Sultan
☎ 2070 3000
✆ 2070 4363

Swiss Inn

(Map B–E5)
Small but comfortable rooms. The location, bang in the centre of Chinatown, is the main attraction and discounts are rare.
✉ 62 Jalan Sultan
☎ 2072 3333
✆ 2031 7799
🖥 www.swissgarden.com

• BUDGET
Pudu Hostel

(Map B–E4)
The best value-for-money hostel in KL, across the road from the bus station and the Star Plaza Rakyat LRT station. A pleasant breakfast area and a choice of dorm beds, singles, doubles and triples. A bar, pool table, laundry, evening meals, luggage storage, and satellite TV. There is a fast Internet connection downstairs.
✉ 3rd Floor, Wisma Lai Choon, 10 Jalan Pudu
☎ 2078 9600
✆ 2070 7377
🖥 www.puduhostel.com

Prices
Budget accommodation is classified here as a room costing less than RM70 per night, and this category includes a private room in a hostel, with a fan or even air conditioning, with attached bathroom. The mid-range category, from RM70 to RM200, will appeal to travellers who want a comfortable room in a hotel, with facilities like a telephone and a kettle in the room and a restaurant on the premises. The luxury category, over RM200, will have all of these plus the full trimmings like a swimming pool, a business centre and a choice of good restaurants. A 5% government tax applies to all hotel rooms, and the fancier establishments will stick on a 10% service charge. A listing of RM200++ (plus plus) refers to the basic room rate excluding the two extra levies.

Backpackers Travellers Inn

(Map B–D4)

The location is fine and even with the cramped space this is a popular budget joint. There is a kitchen, a bar on the roof and films are shown at night.

✉ 60 Jalan Sultan
☎ 2078 2473

Backpackers Travellers Lodge

(Map B–D5)

On a corner opposite the Malaya Hotel, up narrow stairs to the first floor, this is not the most prepossessing hostel in town but it is popular. Rooms lack light and the place is sometimes full; the location, in the heart of Chinatown, helps.

✉ 158 Jalan Tun H.S. Lee
☎ 2031 0889
🖰 btl@tm.net.my

Elsewhere

• LUXURY

Mandarin Oriental

(Map B–G2)

A premier hotel, one of the very best in the city, boasting bars and restaurants that exude style and panache. The service and attention to detail are exemplary.

✉ KLCC
☎ 2380 8888
📠 2380 8803
🖥 www. mandarinoriental.com

Renaissance

(Map B–F2)

A top hotel with an opulent marble lobby, this is a place to seek pampering; excellent facilities and fine restaurants like Marché.

✉ Corner of Jalan Sultan Ismail and Jalan Ampang
☎ 2162 2233
📠 2163 1122
🖥 www. renaissance-kul.com

Hotel Nikko

(Map B–I1)

An imposing hotel close to the Ampang Park LRT station. Part of a Japanese chain and popular with businesspeople. It has a signature Japanese restaurant and an English-style pub.

✉ 165 Jalan Ampang
☎ 2782 6302
🖥 www. hotelnikko.com.my

Shangri-La Hotel

(Map B–F3)

This stylish hotel looks good after its recent facelift. Has water features in the lobby, impeccable restaurants, airy rooms and little extras. Hard to beat.

✉ 11 Jalan Sultan Ismail
☎ 2032 2388
📠 2070 1514
🖥 www. shangri-la.com

Pan Pacific Kuala Lumpur (Map B–C1)

At the top end of Jalan Putra, not quite the centre of city life, but a quality five-star hotel. Tennis courts and pool, first-class restaurants, business-traveller friendly.

✉ Jalan Putra
☎ 4042 5555
📠 4041 7236
🖥 www. panpacific.com

The Legend

(Map B–C1)
Fortress-like building built over The Mall, a large shopping centre. The size (620 rooms) and hybrid Chinese-Renaissance style of the hotel may seem daunting but there are lots of luxuries like an outdoor pool, squash courts, fitness centre, and plenty of restaurants and bars.

✉ *Putra Place, Jalan Putra*
☎ *4142 9888*
📠 *4142 0700*
💻 *www. legendsgroup.com*

Carcosa Seri Negara (Map B–A5)

On the site of the first Resident's home and Britain's official residence in Malaysia till the Japanese arrived in 1941 and took over the place. Now a luxury hotel, its uniqueness is both a strength and a weakness – it attracts dignitaries on very generous expense accounts.

✉ *Taman Tasik Perdana*
☎ *2295 0888*
📠 *2282 6868*
💻 *www. carcosa.com.my*

• MID-RANGE

Heritage Station Hotel (Map B–C5)

The setting is unique, part of the fantastic neo-Moorish railway station that has now been eclipsed by KL Sentral. There are lots of period details but the rooms and facilities are no great shakes. Check it out; the colonial echoes may prove enticing.

✉ *Jalan Sultan Hishamuddin*
☎ *2273 5588*
📠 *2273 2842*

• BUDGET

Coliseum Hotel

(Map B–D3)
This hotel has character. Its history goes back to colonial times when British plantation managers from 'up country' would have a break in the capital, tucking into steaks here for the first time in 1921 (they are still on the menu). The ancient ceiling fans (there is air conditioning) add to the nostalgic feel. The bedrooms and the plumbing are ancient, some rooms have a sink but bathrooms are shared. Can be difficult to get a room so enquire early.

✉ *100 Jalan Tunku Abdul Rahman*
☎ *2692 6270*

Pan Pacific Kuala Lumpur International Airport Hotel (Map A–D6)

If a flight delay results in a stay at the airport hotel, just wheel your trolley over the sky-bridge into the lobby. There are bars and restaurants, a pool, a 24-hour fitness centre, and some rooms have a grand view of the main runway.

✉ *Jalan CTA 4B, KLIASepang*
☎ *8787 3333*
📠 *8787 5555*
💻 *www. panpacific.com*

Above: *One of the delights of street food in KL – satay sticks laid out ready to bite into.*
Below: *In the wet-markets some rather strange delights await the more adventurous eater: thousand-year-old eggs, exotic fruits and sundry strange dried things are all part of classic Chinese cuisine.*

EATING OUT
Where to Eat

Shopping and sightseeing have their roles in life but the real cream on the cake is the food in Kuala Lumpur. Actually, there is very little by way of cream cakes but instead a dazzling, multi-ethnic array of Asian and European cuisines is on offer.

At budget places you can expect to pay less than RM20 for a meal, including a non-alcoholic drink. Mid-range restaurants are where you could expect to choose a main course, perhaps a starter and dessert as well, for between RM20 and RM50, excluding drinks. Luxury places, where a meal for one person without drinks will come to over RM50, mostly cover five-star-hotel restaurants and independent restaurants aspiring to compete with the best.

What to Eat

Chinese cuisine is most likely to be experienced in the form of stir-fried Cantonese dishes, originally from the southern province of Guangdong and now the most common type of Chinese food in Kuala Lumpur. The bite-sized meat and vegetables are cooked quickly in a wok, with the flavour coming from the subtlety of the sauces. Chinese lunch is traditionally made up of dim sum, small snacks that appear on a trolley from which diners point and pick, and look out too for *pau*, steamed rice dumplings with a variety of fillings.

Malay cuisine is home cooking from the *kampung* (village) and restaurants rarely restrict themselves to just Malay cooking. The best way to experience some typical dishes is by way of one of the food courts. Classic dishes include *nasi lemak*, rice cooked in coconut milk, with palate-appealing sauces using lemon grass, chilli, garlic and tamarind.

Indian food tends to be the least expensive cuisine readily available in Kuala Lumpur, and is perfect for vegetarians, as well as anyone seeking a late breakfast. Try *masala dosa*, rice flour pancakes with spicy mashed potato filling and coconut sauce. North Indian cooking provides the more sophisticated side of Indian dining and the Bombay Palace (*see* page 68) is exemplary in this regard.

What to Drink

Drinks of an alcoholic kind are readily available almost everywhere, although the tax makes them more expensive than one would expect. Freshly-made fruit juices are one of the non-alcoholic delights of a visit to Kuala Lumpur and every restaurant and food court should be able to produce a thirst-quenching mix using local fruits. On the streets, look for a sugar cane (*cendol*) stall. Tea (*the*) is a common drink though there is usually little choice of brand and a full teapot of decent tea is rare enough. There is more choice when it comes to coffee (*kopi*), at the designer joints anyway, but local coffee can be strong and condensed milk is frequently added.

Bombay Palace (*see* page 68)

Food Courts

Good value for money (never exceeding the budget price category), a terrific choice of Asian dishes and the comfort of air conditioning help make KL's food courts irresistible. Located above or below shopping malls, they are ideal for a food fix during the throes of a serious shopping expedition. Between meals, they are a good spot for a rest and an iced tea or fresh fruit drink.

One of the best food courts is the one on the top floor of the **KLCC** mall where there are Hainanese chicken rice, *nasi padang*, tom yam, Penang cuisine, northeast Indian cuisine, Asian flavours and *nasi lemak* and *nasi goreng* outlets.

Another good food court is in the **Lot 10 Plaza** at the intersection of Jalan Bukit Bintang and Jalan Sultan Ismail. Also worth a visit is the one on the second level of the **Central Market** in Chinatown. Lacking air conditioning but not uncomfortable is the food plaza in **Sungei Wang** in the Golden Triangle area. There are several Chinese buffet stalls where you just pile up what you want and the owner fixes a price; you won't get cheated.

Right: *You can't get very far along Jalan Bukit Bintang without being drawn into one of its many outdoor coffee shops with their cool customers, vast menus and roaring air conditioners.*

Doing the Bintang Walk

Coffee at a corner pavement café in Paris, a Guinness in an Irish pub – well, Kuala Lumpur's equivalent seems to be an iced coffee and pizza at one of the open-air designer coffee bars that characterize Bintang Walk, complete with machines for blasting cold air onto the seating areas. Bintang Walk is the streetscaped stretch of Jalan Bukit Bintang between the garishly green Lot 10 and the studied elegance of the Ritz-Carlton. Lot 10 is a good place to start a food trail, having a food court of its own serving typical hawker fare, but the trendy joints are strung out along the pavement. Sometimes a table indoors, near a window and away from the traffic, is more comfortable.

The Golden Triangle

• *LUXURY*

OGGI

Meaning 'today' in Italian, OGGI is pleasingly unpretentious in style with white marble floors and tabletops and hidden strip-lighting which changes seamlessly from red to violet to white. Reproductions of Italian Renaissance paintings adorn the walls, although the open kitchen and wood-fire oven is just as eye-catching. There is a wide choice of lunches, from a light pizza and salad to everything on the buffet table plus two main dishes.

✉ *Regent Hotel, 160*

Jalan Bukit Bintang ☎ *2141 8000* 🖳 *www. fourseasons.com*

Shook!

Four open kitchens – Japanese, Chinese, Italian and Western Grill – and the nous to coordinate the arrival of utterly varied dishes to your table. This superb restaurant offers opportunities to combine dishes in unique and surprising ways – a Caesar salad and sashimi works far better together than you ever thought possible – and there is a fine wine list. Better still, the diverse prices allow diners on a mid-range budget to judiciously select an enjoyable lunch or dinner. Recommended. ✉ Starhill Centre, Lower Ground Floor, Jalan Bukit Bintang ☎ 2716 8535 💻 www.ytlcommunity. com/shook

Le Bouchon

Posh-ish setting with white tablecloths and low lighting, and a five-course set meal – goose liver terrine or Burgundy snail with spinach, before a main dish of veal or tiger prawn brochette with Champagne sauce. ✉ L14 & 16, Changkat Bukit Bintang ☎ 2142 7633 💻 www.lebouchon restaurant.com

Shanghai Restaurant

This is the only Shanghainese restaurant in KL. The interior aspires to evoke the stylish city of Shanghai in the 1920s, the 'Paris of the East', with lacquered folding screens, ink paintings of storks, upholstered chairs, crisp white tablecloths

and fine chinaware. The food tends to be meat-based, though dishes like stirfried river prawns in ginger sauce, and white eel with bamboo shoots, are an alternative to pigeon in rice wine or the duck or beef. Lunch and dinner, and Shanghainese dim sum always on tap. ✉ JW Marriott Hotel, Jalan Bukit Bintang ☎ 2716 8288

Eest

Opens in the evening for exciting pan-Asian wonders like lobster tempura for starters, a main course of Cantonese-style beef fillet with foie gras, followed by mango pudding with chocolate and black olive. ✉ The Westin, 199 Jalan Bukit Bintang ☎ 2773 8017

Scalini's

Set upon a quiet hill above the noise of Jalan Sultan Ismail, it is hard to beat the view and the atmosphere if a table in the canopy-covered alfresco

terrace is reserved. Superb Italian food. ✉ 19 Jalan Sultan Ismail ☎ 2145 3211

• MID-RANGE
L'Opera

Easy to find, being next door to Planet Hollywood and opposite the Regent Hotel on Jalan Bukit Bintang. Pizza and pasta dominate the menu and guess what type of Italian music is played in the background? Outdoor tables on the pavement as well as air-conditioned interior. ✉ Wisma Peladang, Bintang Walk ☎ 2144 7808

Bom Brazil Churrascaria

Served from a stainless steel grill heated from above by infra-red, the eat-all-you-can barbecue buffet suits diners with a healthy appetite. Be sure to try everything, especially the hot and cold Brazilian salads, the garlic beef and other choice cuts, lamb with four sauces, and dory

fish fillets.
⊠ *Chankat Bukit Bintang* ☎ *2144 8763*
🕒 *nightly from 18:00*

Lemon Garden 2GO

This is a take-away but with tables and chairs to eat on the spot and people watch. Sandwiches, Japanese sets and salads for a quick lunch fix plus naughty desserts and wine (by the bottle only).
⊠ *Shangri-La Hotel, 11 Jalan Sultan Ismail*
☎ *2032 2388*

Sentidos Tapas

As good a tapas bar as you will find in KL. A cool bar and restrained lighting for a comfortable, away-from-it-all atmosphere. Good food like Caesar salad, seafood paella, deep-fried calamari, baked oysters with shallot confit, sautéed clams in wine. There's tiramisu and crème Catalana, and a range of Spanish wines.
⊠ *Lower Ground Floor, Star Hill Shopping Centre*
☎ *2145 3385*

L'Epicure

European cuisine with an emphasis on the Mediterranean; try the porcini risotto, scallop prawn and the beef cuts. A variety of set lunches, though more of an occasion at night.
⊠ *178 Jalan Imbi*
☎ *2148 8385*

My Thai

Start with drinks in the eye-catching Village Bar, footsteps away, before considering the *som taam goong sod* (papaya salad) or *hoi jor pu* (crabmeat wrapped in tofu) as starters before one of the many curries. Be sure to view the restrooms at some stage of the evening.
⊠ *Lower Ground Floor, STAR Hill Gallery, 181 Jalan Bukit Bintang*
☎ *2148 6151*

Seri Angkasa

Opinions differ as to the quality of the buffet food but there is no disagreement about the exceptional views from this revolving restaurant at the top of the KL Tower, 282m (925ft) high. Open for lunch and dinner, a table for sunset needs advance booking.
⊠ *KL Tower* ☎ *2020 5055* 🖥 *www. serimelayu.com*

Hard Rock Café

Come once to experience the concept, and buy the T-shirt if you must (cheap copies are available in Chinatown's night market in Petaling St). Food is of the up-market fast-food type – gargantuan burgers, nachos, spare ribs – and the décor focuses on music memorabilia.
⊠ *2 Jalan Sultan Ismail*
☎ *2144 4152*

Planet Hollywood

The food is no surprise – burgers, pizza pie, ribs, nachos, chicken, giant sandwiches and strawberry mocktail – but there is a chance of catching an up-and-coming local band.
⊠ *Ground Floor, KL Plaza, 179 Jalan Bukit Bintang* ☎ *2144 6602*

• BUDGET
Restoran Ramzaan

Traditional restaurant where the food is cheap and tasty. Come here for a *roti* and lime juice as a snack, and take a seat by one of the giant fans.

✉ *54 Jalan Bukit Bintang*

Moussandra

Good-value set lunches as well as competitively priced evening meals of pizza, pasta and tapas at this Mediterranean-style restaurant; situated behind the Guardian pharmacy.

✉ *Ground Floor, KL Plaza, Jalan Bukit Bintang*

☎ *2144 0775*

KLCC

The KLCC shopping mall is a gastronomic treat. As well as the trendy restaurants on the 4th floor there are two food malls where a wide choice of tasty Asian meals at budget prices is available.

• MID-RANGE
Al-Marjan

Lebanese and Iranian dishes with tasty appetizers like *mutable* (grilled eggplant) before tucking into a plate of spicy lamb; baklava and laban for desserts.

✉ *Lot 415, 4th Floor, Suria KLCC*

☎ *2168 8557*

Chinatown
• MID-RANGE
Amata

This superb Chinese vegetarian restaurant is worth seeking out. It is a 100-year-old Chinese shophouse, the family well is still there, and the food is a treat. Plenty of 'mock meat' dishes to lure non-vegetarians, like coffee chicken using

Above: *Shopping centres offer goods of all kinds from designer clothes to good food. These people can eat while they watch others spend their hard-earned cash.*

A Food Glossary

There is rarely a language problem when it comes to ordering a meal in a restaurant because English is widely used but it helps to recognize some key terms that appear in the menus at food courts:

nasi • rice
nasi goreng • Malay-style fried rice
mee • noodles
ikan • fish
ayam • chicken
biryani • North Indian spiced rice with meat or vegetables
cendol • Malay dessert using ice shavings over red beans, coloured syrups and coconut milk

---

More food terms

laksa • spicy soup of noodles, bean curd, vegetables and prawns

mee rebus • Malay dish of noodles, potato and hard-boiled egg

murtabak • Indian Muslim pancake bread filled with meat or vegetables

roti • flaky, thin Indian pancake served with a curry sauce

tahu goreng • fried tofu and bean sprouts in peanut sauce, a handy dish for vegetarians

congee • Chinese porridge

Hokkien mee • yellow noodles with slivers of meat, seafood and strips of fried egg

Rending • coconut curry, chicken or beef

dosa • crispy, light pancake

Below: *Chilli crab in one of Chinatown's seafood restaurants is an experience.*

tofu lightly marinated in Nescafé, and special dishes like *bak hup* (lily buds). No alcohol.
✉ *2 Jalan Panggung*
☎ *2026 9077*
🕐 *11:00–22:00*

Wan Fo Yuan

Prices are similar to those at Amata but, although there is air conditioning and a photo-based menu, the restaurant lacks a bit of character. The dishes are authentic, part of a fascinating sub-genre of Chinese cuisine specializing in the culinary cloning of meat dishes for vegetarians who get a kick out of pretending to eat what is taboo.
✉ *8 Jalan Panggung*
☎ *2078 0952*

Naili's Place

Chinatown can get on top of you but try the quiet side of Naili's, facing the hemmed-in river up which Chinese miners came when they founded KL in the 19th century. The food is conventional – pizza, pasta, steak, fish and chips – but there are local dishes like *nasi lemak* and special fried rice to freshen the palate. A bright and friendly, touristy kind of place, with prices at the lower end of the mid-range category.
✉ *Central Market Annexe, Jalan Hong Kasturi*

• *BUDGET*

Restoran Sri Ganesa

Right beside the tiny Ganesh temple, a short walk up the lane that runs by the side of the Puduraya bus station, this little restaurant serves delicious vegetarian dishes which are ideal at lunchtime.
✉ *5 Jalan Pudu Lama*

Restoran Hameed

Located right by Pasir Seni station on the Putra LRT, this breezy restaurant offers a quieter meal than similar kind of establishments around Central Market. Malay and Indian food is cooked daily; in the morning fresh *roti* are rolled out before your eyes. Recommended.
✉ *Jalan Hang Kasturi*

Jalan Doraisamy

Jalan Doraisamy, tucked between Jalan Dang Wangi and Jalan Sultan Ismail, is the latest hi place for wining and dining. Most of the bars and restaurants here stay open after midnight and at weekends the closing time for most of them is 03:00.

• *LUXURY*

Atrium

Dine inside under low-key lighting or outside on the terrace. Fish, grills and pasta dishes make up the menu; lots of expatriates amongst the customers.
✉ *21 Jalan Doraisamy*
☎ *2694 1318*
🖥 *www.atrium.com.my*

That Indian Thing

Indian cuisine with a difference. No simple curries but new-fangled dishes featuring tapas and salads.
✉ *52 Jalan Doraisamy*
☎ *2698 6357* 🖥 *www.thatindianthing.com*

The Ivy

Roast beef with generous helpings of British nostalgia is the main draw in this theme restaurant.
✉ *48 Jalan Doraisamy*
☎ *2693 2260*

Bangsar

Bangsar would be utterly nondescript were it not for the density of innovative, casual-dining eateries. All the restaurants fall into the luxury to mid-range price bracket, depending more on what you eat and less on which restaurant you actually eat in.

Grappa

A trattoria-style restaurant, infectiously likeable, serving tasty pasta, meat, and pizza dishes in a pleasant environment. Italian and Australian wines, also by the glass. Suitable for lunch or dinner, dropping into one of the nearby bars first or later.
✉ *1 Jalan Telawi 5, Bangsar* ☎ *2287 0080*
🖰 *grappa@grappa.com.my*

Le Bodega

A popular restaurant serving light-ish dishes like fried brie and salad, beef stroganoff, steak and mushroom pie. A good drinks list but no real cocktails. Open for breakfast, lunch and dinner.
✉ *16 Jalan Telawi 2, Bangsar* ☎ *2287 8318*
🖥 *www.bodega.com.my*

Chinoz

Beef carpaccio as a starter, oysters flown in live from New Zealand, enticing mezze bar and desserts like

warm chocolate walnut brownies. Stylish food and surroundings.
✉ *8 Jalan Telawi 5, Bangsar* ☎ *2283 1231*

Japanese Dining Bar

Contemporary, new-look Japanese restaurant. A photo menu displays tapas, sushi, sashimi and some 50 types of Japanese liquor. A cool place for chill-out dining, or just drop in for a drink.
✉ *16 Jalan Telawi 5, Bangsar* ☎ *2283 3886*

The Chamber

Wines from Thailand and Japan and food like chilli beef, tom yam, *laksa* and lots of noodle dishes. Cutting-edge Asian décor, with gauze curtains separating the tables.
✉ *33 Telawi 3, Bangsar* ☎ *2283 1898*

Flam's

Sociable restaurant, where prices are more affordable than some of the competition. A catholic menu of meat, fish and pasta dishes.

✉ *16 Jalan Telawi, Bangsar* ☎ *2283 1898*
🖳 *www.flams.com*

Telawi Street Bistro

The quintessential Bangsar restaurant – seared scallops and sea bass gravadlax for starters, venison, lamb or beef as main dish – and the informal air of casual dining. Upstairs is the chill-out area for aperitifs and music.
✉ *1 Jalan Telawi 3, Bangsar* ☎ *2284 3168*

Al Sabeel

Arabic food, no alcohol; dishes include *biryani* lamb, steaks and other grills, and the kitchen's Greek salad.
✉ *2 Jalan Telawi 5, Bangsar* ☎ *2283 2822*

Elsewhere
• *LUXURY*
Marché

The menu at Marché (French for market-place) includes Mediterranean dishes from an innovative young chef, like sole fillet stuffed with lobster, or truffled lamb tartar with chanterelle, and

chocolate ravioli in hot chocolate sauce. Good wine list, attentive service and a comfortable pre-dinner lounge area.
✉ *Renaissance Hotel, corner of Jalan Sultan Ismail and Jalan Ampang* ☎ *2162 2233*
🖳 *www.
renaissance-kul.com*

Top Hat

Graceful dining in an old colonial-era mansion. Enjoy an elegant meal and try the Nyonya (Peranakan) dishes, uncommon outside of Melaka.
✉ *7 Jalan Kia Peng*
☎ *2142 8611*
🕑 *daily 12:00–24:00*

The Gulai House

Part of the imperial Carcosa Seri Negara (see page 21), the cuisine is classic Malay and Indian, in an air of unrestrained luxury.
✉ *Carcosa Seri Negara, Taman Tasik Perdana*
☎ *2282 1888*

• *MID-RANGE*
Bombay Palace

The finest place to

enjoy an Indian meal in KL. North Indian cuisine in a palace setting, with waiters in moghul warrior dress. Vegetarians can share a table with meat eaters. Excellent service.

✉ *388 Jalan Tun Razak*
☎ *245 4241*

Bangles

An Indian tandoori restaurant. The papadums are crisp and minty and the Bhindi Bits, deep-fried slices of okra, delicious. Try the masala dishes served on a hot plate, or the butter chicken or chicken tikka. Wine list, and refreshing jaljeera, cumin-flavoured water sweetened with tamarind.

✉ *270 Jalan Ampang*
☎ *4252 4100* 🖥 *www. bangles.com.my*

Bijan

Malay fine dining in an old bungalow, and a good way to start is the platter of chicken satay, *cucur udang* (prawn fritters), *popiah* (spring rolls) and *tauhu sumbat* (deep-fried

beancurd stuffed with minced prawn and vegetables). Great curries and Malaysian vegetables like wild fern shoots. Cheesecake flavoured with durian, the notoriously smelly but sought-after fruit, for a risky dessert.

✉ *3 Jalan Ceylon*
☎ *2131 3575*

Coliseum

An old hotel and restaurant from the colonial era (*see page 59*); come here to soak up the atmosphere and tuck into one of the hot steaks or baked crab.

✉ *100 Jalan Tunku Abdul Rahman*
☎ *2692 6270*

Below: *Cool, airy and calm, this sidewalk café in one of KL's shopping centres offers a restful break from the heat outside.*

Above: *If the extra-ordinary cuisine of KL tires you out there's always the golden arches to fall back on. Merdeka Square by night.*
Opposite: *Chinese Dragon dancers bring good luck to those they dance for.*

Music in KL
Malaysia has a strong traditional music scene dominated by Sharifah Aini singing Malay ballads. The younger people go for hard rock infused with Malay elements. You can catch some of it on a TV show called *Asia Bagus*. Sheila Majid is Malaysia's biggest pop star. Also listen to the songs of Siti Nurhaliza, closer to the traditional Malay style. What you might encounter live in the city are Indonesian cover bands, or a pretty raunchy music style called Dangdut, sung by Indonesian singers.

ENTERTAINMENT
Nightlife

Kuala Lumpur by night is a very different city to the raging, exhaust-filled business of the daytime. The fairy lights around **Merdeka Square** make the place look more like Disneyland than ever, streets are closed to traffic and the night markets appear, hawker stalls set up all over town, the traffic dies down and families come out to walk the streets in the relative cool of the evening. Above all of it soar the glittering peaks of the **Petronas Towers**, even more imposing at night than during the day.

Good places to stroll around at night are the streets near the Central Market and Petaling Street. Bintang Walk cannot be avoided but if you are in this area walk down Jalan Bukit Bintang and turn right into Changkat Bukit Bintang. The street scene here is informal but safe and there are interesting bars to visit.

If you want something more than an evening stroll or a bit of haggling in a night market there are concerts and the theatre, cultural shows combined with dinner, and a host of street cafés, nightclubs, bars, music clubs and one-off dance events. Most bars and pubs open at lunch time and close around midnight, while the clubs open around 21:00 and stay open till 03:00. Clubs have an entrance fee of around RM20 while a glass of beer will set you back RM8 but look out for happy hours in the pubs in the early evening. Another very popular evening activity in the city is karaoke, ranging from a monitor and sound system in a seedy bar to purpose-built luxury suites which can be hired for the evening.

For information on **what's on** in the city from day to day check out the Metro section of the *Malay Mail*, *The New Straits Times* and *The Star* newspapers.

Theatre

Kuala Lumpur's cultural scene is blooming. The **Panggung Negara** (National Theatre) on Jalan Tun Ismail is a modern purpose-built place with its own theatre company as well as performances by visiting international companies. The building itself is worth the visit for its architecture while inside is an art gallery and restaurants.

Saloma Theatre Restaurant
The Malaysia Tourism Centre is worth a visit just to admire the renovated, colonial-era building that is now its premises and next door to it the Saloma Theatre Restaurant offers a nightly, one-hour performance of cultural dance and music; accompanied by a buffet of Malay food. Start time is 18:30 and the nearest PUTRA station is Dang Wansi, within walking distance.
✉ 139 Jalan Ampang
☎ 2161 0122
🖳 www.saloma.com.my

Music

Classical music is represented in the city by the Petronas Philharmonic Orchestra, based in the **Dewan Philharmonic Theatre** in the Petronas Towers. There are also performances by visiting orchestras in the **Panggung Negara**.

Traditional dance and **music** are most likely to be seen in the various cultural shows put on by restaurants and at the **Central Market**. Some of the restaurant shows are enthusiastic but can be a little tacky. There is also the **Temple of Fine Arts** in Bangsar (*see* page 32) for performances of **Indian dance** and **music**.

Cinema

The city has its full complement of cinemas showing all the latest commercial movies, plus Chinese, Hollywood and Bollywood. Usually the western and Chinese movies are subtitled but the Indian ones tend to be dubbed into Malay.

Festivals

January–February

Thaipusam A Hindu celebration when worshippers, many with their skin pierced by heavy metal frames, make their way to the Batu Caves, accompanying the statue of Lord Subramaniam in his silver chariot.

Federal Territory Day (February 1) Fireworks, streamers, cultural performances, and skydiving off the Petronas Towers.

Chinese New Year (variable) A two-day public holiday marking the first moon of the lunar new year. This is the major celebration for all Chinese people in Kuala Lumpur and most Chinese businesses close

Cinemas

See 🖥 www.cinema.com.my for current information on what is on in the city's cinema.

Golden Screen Cinema,

This is one of the best cinema complexes in the city centre and is easy to reach from Imbi monorail station.
✉ No. 3–109 3rd Level, Berjaya Times Square, Jalan Imbi
☎ 8312 3456
🖥 www.gsc.com.my

Tanjong Golden Village,

This cinema complex in Suria KLCC has a choice of 12 screens. Tickets can be booked in advance; advisable at weekends for the latest Hollywood blockbusters. First film starts at 11:00.
✉ Level 3, Park Mall, Suria KLCC, Jalan Ampang
☎ 7492 2929
🖥 www.tgv.com.my

IMAX Theatre,

A screen five storeys high, with 12,000 watts of digital surround sound; educational themes and Hollywood blockbusters.
✉ Level 510 Berjaya Times Square, Jalan Imbi
☎ 2117 3046
🖥 www.imaxkl.com

MUSIC, CINEMA & FESTIVALS

down for five days. The stalls in Chinatown sell lots of Chinese delicacies and the streets crash to the sounds of the lion dancers and their firecrackers. This is the best time to look for Chinese opera in the streets around Chinatown.

Hari Raya Haji (variable) The celebration of the return of the pilgrims from Mecca. There are lots of activities at the mosques, and families sacrifice a goat and give the meat to the poor.

March–May

Easter (variable) Celebrated quietly by the city's small community of Christians. Chocolate eggs appear in the shops.

Vesak Day (May 25) Celebration of the birth of the Lord Buddha. The Buddhist pagoda in Brickfields comes alive with celebrants who light joss sticks, release caged birds and are given yellow cords by the monks.

Music Venues
Dewan Philharmonic Theatre,
✉ Level 2, Tower 2, Petronas Twin Towers, KLCC
☎ 2051 7007
🖥 www.malaysian philharmonic.com
Note: There is a dress code for performances

Temple of Fine Arts,
✉ 116 Jalan Berhala, Brickfields
☎ 2274 3709

Chinese Opera
Often to be encountered on the streets of the city during Chinese New Year, Chinese Opera is almost incomprehensible to an outsider. It is performed in Cantonese and tells traditional stories in a kind of cross between Gilbert and Sullivan and stand-up comedy. Costumes and make-up are loud, the music is louder still and details such as scenery are left to the imagination. A single performance can take hours but finding one of these amazing events is well worth it.

Left: *One of the huge, elaborately decorated drums common in northern Malaysia, here on display during a drum festival in Merdeka Square.*

Right: *Malaysia is blessed with an abundant and prolific flora. Here some of the country's beautiful plants are on display in the annual flower festival.*

June–August

Yang di-Pertuan Agong's Birthday (7 June) Festivities take place in the city to celebrate the official birthday of the king.

Flower Festival (July, variable) A week-long celebration of Malaysia's plant life culminating in a Floral Parade with flower-covered floats, marching bands, horses and dance troupes.

Festival of the Hungry Ghosts (late August) The night when souls are released from purgatory and walk the streets. Offerings of food and joss sticks appear on makeshift shrines on the street, and there is lots of street opera and much burning of paper money in offerings to the spirits.

National Day (August 31) There are parades in Merdeka Square, and lots of flag waving and speech making. Floats from every state take part, roads around the square are closed and the streets fill with spectators.

September–October

Malaysia Fest A two-week celebration of Malaysian culture. Lots of cultural shows, cooking demonstrations, and exhibitions in hotels. The streets are decorated and the

Public Holidays in
Kuala Lumpur
1 January New Year's Day
Late January/early February Chinese New Year
Late January/early February Hari Raya Haji
1 February Federal Territory Day
February Maal Hijrah
1 May Labour Day
Early May Vesak Day
June (first Saturday) King's birthday
31 August National Day
November Deepavali
November Hari Raya Puasa (2 days)
25 December Christmas Day

shopping malls all compete for the 'best decorated' award.

Mooncake Festival A Chinese festival celebrating the overthrow of the Mongolian Dynasty when, legend has it, the rebels plotted with one another by hiding secret messages in cakes. Mooncakes are given as gifts and the children dress up and carry brightly coloured lanterns.

Nine Emperor Gods Festival The Nine Emperor Gods, who dwell in heaven under the reign of Thean Hou, come to earth for nine days and bring good health and longevity. People visit the temples and eat vegetarian food. The festival ends with a procession to send the nine gods back to the stars.

Deepavali The Hindu festival of light. Hindus celebrate the triumph of good over evil with lights in the temples, and also in their homes, to attract the blessing of the goddess Lakshmi.

Ramadan The month of fasting from dawn till dusk when the streets, especially those around the mosques, come alive with people out enjoying the evening meal.

Hari Raya Puasa The end of the month of fasting. Royal palaces open to the public, people put on new clothes and go out to visit their friends and neighbours, bringing gifts.

Christmas This Christian holiday is celebrated quietly, with Christmas decorations.

A Malay House
Traditional Malay houses are a rapidly vanishing breed in modern KL but they are still to be found (*see* Pak Ali's House page 35). Built entirely from wood they must have evolved over generations in a way which best deals with the humid, wet, and hot climate. Most often up on stilts to create a draught beneath the house and provide storage space, they also have high peaked roofs to reduce the heat of the sun on the building. Fretwork grilles fill the walls for ventilation and long shuttered windows keep out the sun and let in the breeze.

Below: *Mooncakes are an acquired taste but sell by the thousand during the Mooncake festival.*

Wayang Kulit

If you are lucky you may catch an evening performance of the *wayang kulit* (shadow puppet) play while you are in the city. The puppeteer sits hidden behind a screen and manipulates jointed leather puppets whose shadows fall onto the screen. As the puppeteer half sings and half tells the story, traditional instruments accompany him. The *wayang kulit* are more common in the northeast but you should enquire at the tourist office if any shows are planned in the city, especially at the Central Market. Afterwards you can pop into the market and buy your own puppets!

Nightclubs, Bars and Discos

When it comes to nightlife, there is plenty of choice in the **Golden Triangle**:

Frangipani

Where all the beautiful people hang out; mixed clientele, nice cocktails.

✉ *25 Changkat Bukit Bintang* ☎ *2776 2390*
🕐 *21:00–03:00 Fri, Sat*

Finnegan's

Two floors of Irish kitsch, very popular at weekends; wine bar upstairs and Irish things downstairs.

✉ *51/51A Jalan Sultan Ismail* ☎ *2145 1930* 🕐 *11:00 till late, happy hour 12:00–21:00*

Reggae Bar

No prizes for guessing the kind of music played here. The bar is crowded and noisy at weekends when live bands appear, and stays open until 03:00, but the place is more relaxing during weekdays. Beer comes by the glass or jug; women pay less for spirits.

✉ *158 Ground Floor, Jalan H.S. Lee*
☎ *2026 7960*

Mojo

The music is live every Thursday and Sunday night; lively DJs the rest of the week. Pool tables are upstairs while the music and mingling occupies the main bar area by the entrance. A popular place before or after dining in one of the many restaurants on Jalan Doraisamy, open until 03:00.

✉ *42 Jalan Doraisamy*
☎ *2697 7999*

Liquid Bar

Filled to capacity at weekends, when a

mixture of funk, acid and house music livens the place up, a quiet drink can be enjoyed on the open-air Central Market Annexe.

✉ Jalan Hang Kasturi
☎ 2026 5909

Beach Club Café

Commercial chart tunes and gorgeous people; a fun pub and dance club.

✉ 460 Jalan P. Ramlee, Kuala Lumpur
☎ 2166 9919
👤 There is a cover charge for club

Bar Uno

The bar is in the centre of the dance floor; live music at weekends. Drinks cost less during the week but the atmosphere is not as good; closes at midnight. An island-style bar in the middle of the dance floor and a stage for live music at weekends. During weekdays there are often free drinks for women.

✉ 924 Jalan P. Ramlee
☎ 2713 2233

Besides the Golden Triangle, **Bangsar** and **Jalan Ampang** also have clubs:

La Bodega

Live jazz above a tapas bar. This establishemet is less frenetic than the dance clubs.

✉ 18 Jalan Telawi 2, Bangsar

Voyeur

This bar and dance club specializes in House music and R&B.

✉ 11 & 15 Jalan Telawi 2, Bangsar
☎ 2287 8598

Zouk

This is a newly opened branch of the popular Singapore club. The venue consists of the Loft Bar and a drinks terrace, and there is club music. An over-21 age limit applies.

✉ 113 Jalan Ampang
🖥 www. zoukclub.com.my
🕐 21:00–02:00 on weekdays, 21:00–03:00 weekends

Opposite: *KL has come alive in recent years with nightclubs and a flourishing club scene. You can dance till you drop or just hang out and watch the beautiful people.*

Chit Chats

Go anywhere outside of the very built-up areas of the city and you will see the tiny, grotesque lizards known locally as chit chats living in the walls of houses and shops. Stare closely at one and you will see that it is almost transparent, its organs almost glowing through its skin. They sit high up on the walls of houses taking in the heat from the walls and making a strange chattering noise at one another. Occasionally two will decide their territory is being invaded and a great chattering fight will break out. When frightened, the chit chat runs off leaving its tail wriggling behind it. Occasionally you will see one which has managed to grow back a new tail.

Above: *A trishaw driver waits for customers outside Christ Church, Melaka.*

Stadthuys (Museum of Ethnography)
⊠ Dutch Square
⊕ 09:00–18:00 Mon, Wed–Sun; closed Fri 12:15–14:45
💰 RM2

Istana de Sultanan
⊠ Jalan Kota
⊕ 09:00–18:00 daily, closed Fri 12:15–12:45
💰 RM2

Baba-Nyonya Heritage Museum
⊠ 48-50 Jalan Tun Tan Cheng Lock
⊕ daily 10:00–12:30, 14:00–16:30
💰 RM8

Maritime Museum
⊠ Jalan Quayside
⊕ 09:00–18:00 daily, closed Fri 12:15–14:45, closed Tue
💰 RM2

Boat Trips
⊠ Tourist office jetty
🖥 www.melaka.net
⊕ Hourly, 10:00–12:00
💰 RM8

EXCURSIONS
Melaka

Slumbering around the banks of the Sungei Melaka this city deserves a visit for its architectural heritage, its unspoiled Chinatown, its Peranakan and Portuguese culture, and its sleepy laid-back atmosphere.

In the heart of the city on the east side of the river is the old **Dutch quarter** with brick-red painted 17th-century buildings. The **Stadthuys**, once the town hall, is now the **Museum of Ethnography**, with displays of Chinese and Malay ceramics, weapons and a reconstruction of a Dutch dining room. Beside the Stadthuys is **Christ Church** with its lovely simple interior, built in 1753, again by the Dutch. Two more old churches are worth visiting in the city – **St Peter's Catholic Church**, the oldest in Malaysia and cultural centre for the descendants of the Portuguese who once held the city, and **St Francis Xavier's**, a much later 19th-century building.

Around the colonial core of the city there are several **museums**. Best of them is the **Istana**, a modern reconstruction of the Malay Palace where the rulers of the city once lived. The building is beautiful, more so than the contents which include displays of ancient court life and illustrations of the stories of Melaka's famous heroes: Hang Tuah, Hang Jebat and Hang Kasturi.

Another good place to visit in the city is **Bukit St Paul**, a strenuous scramble with the shell of the 16th-century **St Paul's** church on the top. At the foot of the hill is the **Porta de Santiago**, all that is left of a massive fort built by the Portuguese, the city's original conquerors. The fort lasted for 296 years until the British blew it up in 1807.

MELAKA

Best of all in Melaka is **Chinatown**, on the west side of the river, where the original street plan is in place and the streets are filled with curio shops and cafés. Here also is the privately owned **Baba-Nyonya** museum, filled with 19th-century domestic fixtures and paraphernalia in a house where all the original architecture is in place. The Peranakan culture emerged here in Melaka and in Singapore as Chinese immigrants, grown wealthy from trade, took Malay wives and developed this hybrid culture of archaic Chinese customs, Malay cooking techniques and British decorations. Chinatown has its fill of ancient temples and mosques, including **Masjid Kampung Hulu**, thought to be the oldest mosque in Malaysia.

An easier, more relaxing way to see the city is by boat. From the tourist office, boats make the journey along the tranquil Melaka River and give a very different perspective of the city. On its return journey the boat goes out to the river mouth where wooden trading ships moor and the **Maritime Museum** is situated.

In the evenings the area around the **Padang** is the venue for a sound and light show which tells the history of Melaka as it lights up the various parts of the city.

Melaka
Location: Map E
Distance from KL: 144km (93 miles)
🚌 Express buses hourly from Pudu Raya Bus Station

The Story of Hang Tuah and Hang Jebat
In the ancient Malay court, tells the 17th-century epic poem *Hikayat Hang Tuah*, were three swashbuckling friends who were trained in the Malay martial arts. After brilliantly saving the life of a court official they were made favourites at court, especially Hang Tuah. Jealous court officials put it about that Tuah had seduced the sultan's consort and the sultan ordered his death. Tuah hid away but when his friend, Jebat, heard he was dead he ran amok in the city, slaughtering many people. Fearing for his own life the sultan turned to Hang Tuah, who had come out of hiding, and told him to kill his friend. Out of loyalty to the sultan Tuah did as he was ordered and the two fought an epic battle in which Hang Jebat was killed.

Left: *All that remains of St Paul's Church on Bukit St Paul, Melaka.*

Taman Negara
Location: Map D
Distance from KL:
400km (250 miles)

Taman Negara Resort
✉ Kuala Tahan
☎ 09 266 3500
🍽 Two restaurants at the resort and more at Kuala Tahan.

Malaysian Tourism Centre
✉ 109 Jalan Ampang
☎ 2164 3929
🕘 09:00–21:00 daily

Nusa Camp
✉ SPKG Tours, Jerantut
☎ 09 266 2369
📧 spkg@tm.net.my
🍽 One cafeteria

Pangolins
More commonly known as the scaly anteater, pangolins are common animals in the rural areas of Malaysia and can be seen in Taman Negara. They feed on termites and use their strong claws to break open termite nests. When threatened they roll up into a ball.

Taman Negara

Less of an excursion and more of an adventure, Taman Negara is the best place to visit in Malaysia for its amazing wildlife, white water river trips, the stunning sights and sounds of the rainforest and the chance to meet some Orang Asli. This is not a trip for the fainthearted: strong boots, insect repellent and the ability to see the funny side of leeches are essential requirements.

The pleasure starts before you even get there. The first part of the journey is by bus or car to Tembeling where a 2–3 hour **boat ride** begins. This has to be one of the best journeys to a holiday destination anywhere. The old wooden boats, driven by outboard engines, creak their way upriver, past *kampungs* with children playing and people doing their washing. Water buffalo loom out of the water and hornbills cruise overhead, giving sarcastic honks as they pass.

The park headquarters at **Kuala Tahan** has become a bit too glossily expensive in recent years, pricing a lot of visitors out of the market. But you can stay at the cheaper places on the other side of the river and still enjoy all the benefits of a trip to a rainforest.

At 4343km² (1676 sq miles), Taman Negara is the largest tract of **rainforest** in Malaysia and much of it is the oldest rainforest in the

world, around 130 million years old. Large parts of it have never been logged, and much of it has been protected since 1925, originally as a game reserve for the colonials. There are wild elephants and tigers in the forest though you'd be very lucky indeed to see one of them. For a long time the park really was a wild place to visit but since 1991 the main accommodation has been privatized, with all the concomitant commercialism that that involves.

Once you are there, arrange a river trip, a night out in a hide in the jungle, some walks into the rainforest and a visit to the canopy walkway where you are up in the trees and can see the rainforest from a very different perspective. One idea if you don't like the too-commercially minded hotel is to arrange a stay at **Nusa camp** a little way upriver from the resort. From here you can climb **Gunung Warisan** or walk to the **Abai waterfall**.

You should certainly see some **wildlife** while you are at Taman Negara, and a night walk with a guide is highly recommended. Huge monitor lizards forage around the edges of the headquarters for food, deer and macaques come close to the buildings, and the insects get everywhere. Along the walking paths, depending on how wet it is, be prepared to encounter leeches and great showers of butterflies that are attracted to the sweat on your T-shirt. The best thing of all is to walk along one of the forest trails for a while and then just stand and listen; the noise of all those creatures going about their business can be quite soul-stirring.

Orang Asli (*see* panel, page 37) live within the park and it is not unusual to see them on the river in hollowed out canoes, using blow pipes to catch their lunch.

As an alternative to the rather expensive hotel at park headquarters, visit the Hotel Malaya in Chinatown (*see* page 57) where there is a desk with details of alternative accommodation and package deals.

Above: *One of the greatest pleasures of Taman Negara is the boat ride into the reserve.*
Opposite: *A canopy walkway through the rainforest.*

Accommodation in the Park

Inside the park itself accommodation is organized by the Taman Negara resort. It consists of expensive dormitory accommodation, chalets and bungalows. A cheaper option is to stay at one of the hotels or home-stays across the river at Kuala Tahan. At Nusa Camp, further upriver, there is a very basic collection of bungalows, chalets and dormitory accommodation.

You must book in advance, either with the resort itself, at the Malaysian Tourism Centre (for Nusa Camp or the resort) in Jalan Ampang, or through a travel agent.

Kuala Selangor

Some 67km (42 miles) northwest of KL is this former royal town on the banks of the River Selangor. It's worth the trip for the amazing little **nature park** in the locality and the further night trip to the tiny village of Kampung Kuantan to see the fireflies. The town itself has some good seafood restaurants and if you have time to spare you could go and visit **Fort Altingberg**, all that remains from when local sultans fought for control of the area's tin mines.

The **nature park** is 2km (1.25 miles) from the town and includes reclaimed **mangrove** swamps, the nearest and most accessible to Kuala Lumpur. These are strange places with trees rearing up out of the salt water of the river estuary. Along the well-marked forest trails are observation huts where you may be able to spot some of the wildlife, including the ubiquitous red crab.

Kampung Kuantan is the real highlight of the trip. Just 8km (5 miles) inland from Kuala Selangor it is the stepping off point for an evening trip along the Selangor River to see the hordes of **fireflies** which hover around the river, strangely flashing synchronously. They are best seen between 20:00 and 22:00.

The whole experience has been highly organized in recent years and a **resort hotel** has opened up in Kampung Kuantan. Otherwise there are companies in KL who arrange a day trip to take in all three sights. Doing the trip by public transport is difficult since there are no buses to Kampung Kuantan and a taxi from KL is expensive – it will cost RM100 or more.

Kuala Selangor
Location: Map C–B4
Distance from KL:
67km (42 miles)
🚌 Bus 141 from Pudu Raya Bus Station
🍴 Seafood restaurants in town.

Kuala Selangor
Nature Park
☎ 3289 2294
🕐 08:00–19:00
💰 Free
🍴 No food available in the park.

Firefly Park Resort
✉ Kampung Kuantan
☎ 2389 1208
🖥 www.fireflypark.com
🕐 daily 07:45–22:30
💰 Boats: RM10 per person, minimum 2 people. Accommodation: RM50 per person
🍴 No food available in the village.

Backpackers Transport
☎ 2032 1988
💰 RM150 including fireflies, nature park, dinner, return trip.

The Cameron Highlands

Discovered by the colonials in the late 19th century and developed as a hill station from the 1920s, the Cameron Highlands are a blessed retreat from the humidity and heat of the city. The **climate** is altogether different from that of the rest of Malaysia. Here you will see honeysuckle, potatoes and strawberries growing alongside roses and tea in a pretty mountain setting. The place was developed largely by wealthy English people who built their dream mock-Tudor homes here as a place to get away from it all. The original inhabitants of this idyllic mountain setting, the Orang Asli, still live here but nowadays they sell blowpipes and other artefacts to the tourists rather than using them.

At weekends people come here in droves from the city so it is best to travel here mid-week but even at weekends the mountain pathways are deserted and the place hasn't succumbed yet to the noisy nightlife of some of the other hill stations.

A great place to visit while you are here is a tea plantation where tea is picked and packaged. There are vegetable farms to visit as well as a butterfly farm and rose gardens. There are two good hotels to visit for afternoon tea and scones – the **Lakehouse** at Ringlet and the **Smokehouse** at Tanah Rata. Both have been converted from old mansions and they are full of the atmosphere of bygone days.

Cameron Highlands
Location: Map F
Distance from KL:
150km (93 miles)

Boh Tea Estate
⊠ Ringlet, Cameron Highlands
🕑 11:00–15:00
Tue–Sun
👣 Free

The Lakehouse
⊠ Ringlet, Cameron Highlands
☎ 05 495 6152
🖥 www.lakehouse-cameron.com

The Smokehouse Hotel
⊠ Tanah Rata
☎ 05 491 1215
🖥 www.thesmokehouse.com

Opposite: *One of the denizens of the mangrove swamps, this red crab makes its home in the aerial roots of the mangrove trees.*
Below: *The tea drinker's heaven – tea plantations as far as the eye can see.*

Above: *Driving in KL can be a very special experience. Lane discipline can seem lax and in the city itself gridlock is always a possibility. Once out of the city, however, the roads are good and the driving is easy.*

Street Signs in Malay

It is very unlikely that you will come across signs that aren't bilingual but here are some Malay signs:

Keluar • Exit
Masuk • Entrance
Pertanyaan • Information
Tutup • Closed
Buka • Open
Awas • Danger
Bahaya • Danger
Balai polis • Police station
Tandas • Toilets
Lelaki • Men
Perempuan • Women
Tarik • Pull
Tolak • Push
Apotik/Farmaci • Chemist/Pharmacy
Doktor gigi • Dentist

Best Times to Visit

Being close to the equator Kuala Lumpur really has no seasons to speak of. Temperatures in the city are a fairly constant 30°C (86°F), falling slightly in the evening and after a rainfall, and humidity is constantly high. If your visit is just to the city then weather really isn't a factor, but if you mean to visit other parts of the country you should bear in mind that from December to late February Malaysia has a rainy season that affects the east coast and can have an effect on places such as Taman Negara. If you are just visiting the city, the early part of the year is best for all the festivals. Be aware also of the school holidays when the tourist attractions can get very crowded.

Tourist Information

There are several good tourist information centres in the city and one at KLIA Airport. They offer tourist information, good useable maps of the city, bookings for some of the city hotels and also some resorts outside of the city, long-distance bus journeys and tours, and car rental.

For information on events and listings look for the free magazine *Juice* or the entertainment sections in the *Sun* and the *Malay Mail*.

Malaysian Tourist Offices in KL:

✉ 109 Jalan Ampang,
☎ 2164 3929,
🖥 www.mtc.gov.my
🕐 24 hours.
✉ Level 1, KL Sentral,
☎ 2272 5828,
🕐 09:00–18:00.
✉ Arrivals Hall, KLIA,
🕐 09:00–21:00.

**Malaysian Tourist
Offices Abroad:**
Australia
✉ Ground Floor,
MAS Building,
William St, Perth,
☎ 09 9481 0400.
Canada
✉ 830 Burrard St,
Vancouver, BC V6Z
2K4, ☎ 04 689 8899,
🖰 mtpb-yvr@msn.com
United Kingdom
✉ 57 Trafalgar
Square, London WC2N
5DU, ☎ 020 7930
7932, 🖰 info@
Malaysia.org.uk.
United States
✉ Suite 810,
120 E. 56th St,
New York, NY10022,
☎ 212 754 1113

Entry Requirements

Most nationalities on
entering Malaysia with
a valid passport are
given a 30- or 60-day
visa on arrival. This can
easily be extended by
applying at the
Immigration Depart-
ment. You should note
that if you wish to trav-
el on to Sarawak you
need a further entry
stamp which allows
you to remain for one
month and which can
be extended further.
Immigration Office:
✉ Block 1 Pusat
Bandar Damansara,
☎ 255 5077.
**Embassies and
Consulates:**
Australia
✉ 6 Jalan Yap Kwan
Seng, ☎ 2146 5555.
Canada
✉ 17th Floor, Menara
Tan & Tan, 207 Jalan
Tun Razak,
☎ 2718 3333.
France
✉ 196 Jalan Ampang,
☎ 2053 5500.
Germany
✉ 26th Floor, Menara
Tan & Tan, 207 Jalan
Tun Razak,
☎ 2170 9666.
United Kingdom
✉ 185 Jalan Ampang,
☎ 2170 2360.
United States
✉ 376 Jalan Tun
Razak, ☎ 2168 5000.

Customs

Visitors to Malaysia
are allowed to bring
into the country for
their personal use 200
cigarettes, 50 cigars or
250g of tobacco and
1 litre of alcohol. In
addition there is no
duty on electrical
goods, cameras,
watches, cosmetics
and perfumes.

Health
Requirements

It is highly recommend-
ed that you take out
travel insurance in your
home country for the
duration of your stay in
the city. This must
include theft or loss of
property and money
and health cover. In
addition, if you plan to
travel to Taman Negara
or undertake any dan-
gerous activities you
should ensure that
these are covered by
your insurance policy.
In the unlikely event
of you needing to
make a claim, you need
some documentation
such as hospital bills or
a police report.
While there are no
essential inoculation
requirements for entry
to Malaysia, it is
important that visitors
are protected against
hepatitis A, polio and
typhoid. You should
also note that it is pos-

sible to catch malaria, Japanese B encephalitis and dengue fever through mosquito bites. In KL this is relatively unlikely although there have been deaths in the Kuala Lumpur area from dengue fever in recent years. You should carry, and use if necessary, mosquito repellent. In rural areas there is also the possibility of rabies.

Getting There by Air

From the **United Kingdom**, there are frequent non-stop flights from London and Manchester to Kuala Lumpur with a flight time of around 13 hours. With the big carriers such as Malaysia Airlines the cheapest flights are Apex, bookable 21 days in advance and carrying a cancellation fee. Cheaper flights with companies such as Qantas, KLM, Turkish Airlines or Gulf Air can involve a much longer journey

with stopovers.

Major Airlines in the United Kingdom:
British Airways
🖥 www.ba.com
Emirates
🖥 www.emirates.com
Malaysia Airlines
🖥 www.malaysia-airlines.com
Singapore Airlines
🖥 www.singaporeair.com
Qantas
🖥 www.qantas.com
From the east coast of the **USA** and **Canada** flight time is about 21 hours and always involves a stopover. From the west coast of the USA flight time is about 19 hours. Malaysia Airlines is the only carrier operating direct flights to Kuala Lumpur from North America: from Los Angeles with a stopover in Tokyo or Taipei, and from New York with a stopover in Dubai. Singapore Airlines has a stopover in Singapore. Carriers such as Korean Air do cheaper, but longer flights. From Canada, Air

Canada flies to Hong Kong, Seoul or Tokyo and arranges onward flights with other carriers. Korean Air flies from Vancouver to KL with a connection in Seoul.

Major Airlines in North America:
Air Canada
🖥 www.aircanada.com
Air France
🖥 www.airfrance.com
Cathay Pacific
🖥 www.cathaypacific.com
Connections from **Australia** and **New Zealand** are frequent and managed by several airlines including all three national carriers. Here especially it is a good idea to shop around for the lowest prices.
From all three regions open-jaw arrangements are possible, allowing you to fly into KL and return from a different city.
KLIA Airport, the gorgeous new international airport, is at Sepang, 72km (46 miles) south of the city. At the arrivals

hall are car hire stands, a money changing facility (traveller's cheques during office hours only), a left luggage office, a post office and a tourist office. There are also several places to eat including a food court doing reasonable local food. The quickest way into KL is by the **KLIA Express** train from Level 1, terminating at KL Sentral from where a **taxi** or **local LRT** takes you to your city destination. Alternatively there are **airport coaches** from the bus station on Level 1 which drop off passengers at their hotel. **Taxis** also ply the route between the airport and the city. Tickets are bought in advance in the Arrivals Hall. For four people a taxi should be cheaper than the bus.

What to Pack

Take as little as possible with you. Anything you plan to buy for your trip –

shoes, clothes, medicines, spectacles, even luggage – is almost certainly cheaper in KL and you have to plan space for all the things that you will buy when you get there. Clothes and shoes should be as lightweight as possible but avoid synthetics – cotton is best for the humidity. A cardigan is a good idea for your hotel room and restaurants as well as the trip into the mountains. Books are expensive in Malaysia so bring a novel and be prepared to trade when you have finished it. Umbrellas can be bought in the city and discarded, and mackintoshes are of very little use in the heat.

Money Matters

Currency: The unit of currency is the Malaysian Ringgit, written RM on price tags but usually called a dollar in conversation. It is divided into 100 sen. Notes are

> **Malaysian Customs and Etiquette**
> There are a few rules the unwary visitor might need to know:
> • On arrival at someone's home you will notice a collection of shoes at the front door. This is because Malaysians always remove their shoes before entering someone's house. It would be insulting not to.
> • Another area of sensitivity is touch. Muslims in particular avoid contact with unfamiliar members of the opposite sex so hesitate before offering to shake hands – if the other person is willing to do this they will let you know. The left hand is never used in social occasions by Malays – never use it to eat, pick up food or offer your left hand to someone.
> • The feet are also a taboo area in Malay society. Never raise them towards someone or point with your foot.
> • Chinese people do not put their chopsticks into their mouths. Neither do they put them into shared food dishes – use a serving spoon. Particularly don't stick chopsticks into the communal bowl of rice if there is one – it's very unlucky.
> • New money at the end of a working day is especially good luck to a Chinese person so if you are buying something in a Chinese shop and want to please them, use new notes and buy late.

Further Reading
• **Anthony Burgess**
The Long Day Wanes.
Trilogy of novels set in
1950s Malaya.
• **Margaret Shennan**
Out in the Midday Sun.
A picture of life in the
days of the British
Empire in Malaya
written by one of the
planters' wives.
• **Roy Follows** *The*
Jungle Beat. The story
of a British policeman
in the jungles of Malaya
in the communist insur-
gency of the 1950s.
• **K S Maniam** *The*
Return; In a Far
Country. Funny, wry
account of life in
Malaysia by an Indian
Malaysian.
• **Chin Kee Onn**
Malay Upside Down.
The impact of the
wartime Japanese
occupation of Malaya.
• **Salleh Ben Joned**
As I Please. If you only
read one book read
this one – a collection
of newspaper articles
by an outspoken and
proud Malaysian.
• **John Briggs** *Parks*
of Malaysia. Essential
reading if you plan to
visit Taman Negara or
some of the other
wildlife areas of the
country.
• **Heidi Muran** *Culture*
Shock! Malaysia. All
the things you need to
know in order to avoid
offence in KL.

RM1, 2, 5, 10, 20, 50 and 100. Coins are 1 sen, 5 sen, 10 sen, 20 sen, 50 sen and RM1. The ringgit tends to follow the fortunes of the US dollar. Exchange rates are posted at all banks and exchange booths. There is no black market in Malaysian currency.

Traveller's cheques in sterling and dollars are accepted at banks and exchange booths as well as some hotels upon presentation of your passport. The best exchange rates are in exchange booths. Major **credit cards** are accepted in the more expensive hotels, shops and restaurants. Using your **bank card**, you should be able to withdraw cash from ATMs (automatic tel- ler machines), readily available throughout the city and open 24 hours, and this is a very convenient and safe way to manage your money. **Banking hours** are Monday to Friday 10:00–16:00, Saturday 09:30–11:30. Money-changers are open during business hours and often late into the evening. Most department stores have fixed prices but in the markets, some of the cheaper hotels and in some of the shopping malls, particularly those that sell com- puter software and electronics, bargain- ing is essential. Think in terms of about a third of the price the stallholder originally asks for. If they agree to a price at once you have offered too much.

City Transport

Although the city centre with most of the major sights is easy enough to walk around, the city's **light rail system** or a **bus** is a far better means of transport, especially if you are not used to the cli- mate. Even one or two stops give you a five-minute break in icy air conditioning which will revive you for some more walking. On the street do not rely on traffic lights since motorbikes in particular tend to ignore them. When using public transport remember that the rush hours are around 08:00–10:00 and 16:30–18:30.

The Metro: It is hard to appreciate just how wonderful the three metro systems are unless you lived in KL before they were built. The three lines cover most of the places you are likely to visit but, surrendering to market forces instead of developing what could have been one of the world's most streamlined and seamless urban transport systems, they fail to link up properly and visitors must often leave one system and board the train of another in order to reach their destination. At one interchange, travellers must leave the station and cross a busy road to enter the other system's station. It is easy to find the nearest metro station in the city centre since all you have to do is follow the overhead monorail lines till you arrive at a stop. Trains run from 06:00 to midnight and fares range from 80 sen. On the **Star line** you can buy stored value tickets but these do not work on the other systems where you pay in advance and pass your ticket through an automatic gate. There are also two commuter lines linking the suburbs with the city but visitors staying around the city area are not likely to use them.

Buses are cheap and mostly air conditioned but are difficult to familiarize yourself with on a short trip.

Taxis are a better option and are relatively inexpensive but you can queue for a long time for one even at off-peak times. In busy periods cabs have a tendency to go out of the city centre to avoid gridlocked streets. Fares start at RM2 for the first 2km and increase by 10 sen every 200 metres. All **city cabs** are metered but check that the driver sets the meter when you get in. Prices for **long-distance taxis** must be negotiated before you get in.

Business Hours

Banks: 09:30–16:00 Mon–Fri, 09:30–11:30 alternate Saturdays. **Government offices:** 08:00–12:45 and 14:00–16:15 Mon–Fri, 08:00–12:45 Sat. **Shops:** 09:30–19:00. **Shopping Centres:** 10:00–22:00.

Time Difference

Malaysia is 8 hours ahead of Greenwich Mean Time, 16 hours ahead of Pacific Standard Time, 13 hours ahead of Eastern Standard Time, and 2 hours behind Sydney, Australia.

Telephone Numbers
The city code for Kuala Lumpur is 03. Add this to the telephone number if dialing from outside the city.

A Serious Warning
In Malaysia there is a mandatory **death sentence** for possession of what in other countries would be considered quite small quantities of drugs. The law in Malaysia makes no distinction between what in the west are termed 'hard' and 'soft' drugs. Anyone, even a foreign tourist, found in possession of drugs of any kind can expect at best an extremely long prison sentence in a foreign jail and at worst execution by hanging.

A Medical Kit
While all of the items on this list are easily available from shops all over the city, if you are planning on making any of the excursions to rural spots it is best to carry some form of medical kit:
- Mild painkiller
- Antihistamine tablets
- Antiseptic cream
- Antifungal cream
- Band-aids
- Immodium or Lomotil for stomach upsets
- Dioralyte powders for dehydration
- Mosquito repellent
- Lip balm
- Suntan lotion
- Travel sickness pills.

Personal Safety

Kuala Lumpur is one of the safest cities in Southeast Asia. As is the case in any other city, however, visitors should be careful with their cash and valuables, keeping them in their sight and if possible in money belts. There are pickpockets in the city as in all other cities, and a particular problem in KL is purse snatching by motorcyclists, so handbags should always be carried on the side away from the road. Only use credit cards in bona fide places (although nowadays even that is no guarantee against credit card fraud anywhere in the world). If you are staying in budget accommodation, a sturdy padlock for your luggage is a good idea. It goes without saying that women in particular should avoid all the places they might choose to avoid in their own city.

Keeping Healthy

In the high humidity of Kuala Lumpur even very small cuts can become infected if not looked after properly. Fungal infections are common and it is best to wear flip flops even in the shower. Prickly heat is a common fungal infection and can be treated with prickly heat powder. For thrush, antibiotic creams such as Canesten are available over the counter in pharmacies. Sunburn and dehydration are easily protected against by drinking plenty of fluids, keeping out of the sun as much as possible and using a good sunscreen with a high sun protection factor. A sunhat is both sensible and pretty, and so are sunglasses. Bear in mind that alcohol can add to a dehydration problem rather than improve it. Tap water is safe to drink in KL but is unpleasant.

However, bottled mineral water is available everywhere. Food poisoning and an upset stomach are also a consideration in this part of the world, although even at streetside stalls the food is freshly cooked and so there is little chance of contracting an infection. You should wash all fresh fruit, avoid food which is kept warm in heated trays, and wash your hands regularly. Remember that unfamiliar food can also bring on bouts of indigestion and upset stomach. Having said all that, bear in mind that most people return home from 'darkest' Malaysia in a state of good health and much happier than when they left home!

Emergencies

In an emergency dial ☎ **999** for the **police** and ☎ **994** for an **ambulance** or the **fire brigade**. There is a special **tourist police**

office in Kuala Lumpur: ☎ 2146 0522 or 2163 3657.

Kuala Lumpur General Hospital: ✉ Jalan Pahang, ☎ 2962 1044.

Tung Shin Hospital: ✉ 102 Jalan Pudu, ☎ 2072 1655.

Twin Towers Medical Centre: ✉ Lot 402, Level 4, Suria KLCC, ☎ 2382 3500.

Language

The official national language of Malaysia is Bahasa Malaysia, or Malay. In Malaysian schools the students learn their subjects through the medium of Malay but they also learn their own mother tongue as well as English, which has become the language of business once again after a long period of being discouraged. Any effort to speak Malay will be greatly appreciated by the locals and some terms are useful if only for ordering your lunch.

Some Useful Words and Phrases

selamat pagi • good morning
selamat petang • good afternoon
selamat malam • good evening
tidak • no
tolong • please
terimah kaseh • thank you
maaf • sorry, pardon me, excuse me
apa khabar • how are you?
baik • good
tidak baik • no good
do mana...? • where is...?
pangil doktor • call a doctor
pangil ambulans • call an ambulance
saya I • I am
saya tidak fahan • I don't understand
saya dirompak • I've been robbed
saya lelah • I am asthmatic
saya kencing manis • I am diabetic
saya hamil • I am pregnant
saya alergik kepada ... • I'm allergic to ...
antibiotik • antibiotics
aspirin • aspirin
penisilin • penicillin
kacang • nuts
lebah • bees
sipakah? • who?
apa? • what?
bilakah? • when?
di mana? • where?
berapa? • how?
pukul berapakah ... berangkat? • what time does the ... leave?
bas • bus
kapal terbang • plane
kapal • ship
keretapi • train

INDEX OF SIGHTS

General Index

Page numbers given in **bold** type indicate photographs

GENERAL INDEX

GENERAL INDEX

GENERAL INDEX